THE MATERIAL WORLD OF ANCIENT EGYPT

The Material World of Ancient Egypt examines the objects and artifacts, the representations in art, and the examples of documentation that together reveal the day-to-day physical substance of life in ancient Egypt. This book investigates how people dressed, what they ate, the houses they built, the games they played, and the tools they used, among many other aspects of daily life, paying great attention to the change and development of each area within the conservative Egyptian society. More than any other ancient civilization, the ancient Egyptians have left us with a wealth of evidence about their daily lives in the form of perishable objects, from leather sandals to feather fans, from detailed depictions of trades and crafts on the walls of tombs and a wide range of documentary evidence from temple inventories to personal laundry lists. Drawing on these diverse sources and richly illustrating his account with nearly one hundred images, William H. Peck illuminates the culture of the ancient Egyptians from the standpoint of the basic materials they employed to make life possible and perhaps even enjoyable.

William H. Peck is retired curator of ancient art at the Detroit Institute of Arts. He excavated for many years in Egypt, first as a field archaeologist at the site of ancient Mendes in the Nile delta and later in the Precinct of the Goddess Mut in Karnak, where he was co–field director and architect with the Brooklyn Museum mission. He was a recipient of an American Research Center in Egypt Fellowship to study New Kingdom tomb painting, a Smithsonian Institution Travel Grant to Egypt, and an Award in the Arts for an outstanding alumnus from Wayne State University. His major publications include *Drawings from Ancient Egypt*, which was translated into French, German, and Arabic; *Splendors of Ancient Egypt*, an exhibition catalog; and *Egypt in Toledo*, on the Egyptian collections in Toledo, Ohio. He has lectured widely in the United States and Canada and has acted as consultant to several museums, including the Virginia Museum, Richmond; the Arkansas Art Center, Little Rock; and the Art Museum, Toledo.

The Material World of Ancient Egypt

WILLIAM H. PECK

University of Michigan–Dearborn

CAMBRIDGE
UNIVERSITY PRESS

Shaftesbury Road, Cambridge CB2 8EA, United Kingdom

One Liberty Plaza, 20th Floor, New York, NY 10006, USA

477 Williamstown Road, Port Melbourne, VIC 3207, Australia

314–321, 3rd Floor, Plot 3, Splendor Forum, Jasola District Centre, New Delhi – 110025, India

103 Penang Road, #05–06/07, Visioncrest Commercial, Singapore 238467

Cambridge University Press is part of Cambridge University Press & Assessment, a department of the University of Cambridge.

We share the University's mission to contribute to society through the pursuit of education, learning and research at the highest international levels of excellence.

www.cambridge.org
Information on this title: www.cambridge.org/9780521713795

First published 2013

A catalogue record for this publication is available from the British Library

Library of Congress Cataloging-in-Publication data
Peck, William H., 1932–
The material world of ancient Egypt / William H. Peck, University of Michigan–Dearborn.
    pages.   cm.
Includes bibliographical references and index.
ISBN 978-0-521-88616-1 (hardback) – ISBN 978-0-521-71379-5 (pbk.)
1. Egypt – Antiquities.   2. Art, Egyptian.   3. Material culture – Egypt.
4. Egypt – Social life and customs.   5. Egypt – Civilization – To 332 B.C.
6. Egypt – Civilization – 332 B.C.–638 A.D.   I. .Title.
DT61.P43   2013
932–dc23   2012046781

ISBN   978-0-521-88616-1   Hardback
ISBN   978-0-521-71379-5   Paperback

CONTENTS

FIGURES

PREFACE

My interest in ancient Egypt began early in my childhood and became more intense during my secondary school years when I discovered Piazzi-Smyth's *Our Inheritance in the Great Pyramid*. I eventually sought to know more about the culture of Egypt as it was preserved in its own artifacts, somewhat in the way that Flinders Petrie was to debunk Piazzi-Smyth's famous work by accurately measuring the monuments. After experience in the U.S. Army as a topographic surveyor and a technical illustrator I was privileged to participate at length in two major excavations, first at the site of Mendes in the Nile delta and later in the Precinct of the Goddess Mut at Karnak. Those activities, my lengthy museum experience of dealing firsthand with a wide range of Egyptian artifacts, and an early involvement with the investigation of mummies as a founding member and participant in the just-emerging Paleopathology Society have given me a series of varied and immediate experiences in the art and objects that make up the material world of ancient Egypt.

ACKNOWLEDGMENTS

The historical list of scholars I am personally indebted to must include William Stevenson Smith, Henry George Fischer, Nicholas B. Millet, Edward L. B. Terrace, Bernard V. Bother, and Donald P. Hansen. Each of these distinguished Egyptologists and scholars encouraged me at some time in my career or contributed in some way to my professional development. Richard A. Fazzini and Jacobus van Dijk, colleagues in the Brooklyn Museum excavation at the Precinct of the Goddess Mut at Karnak, have offered continued support and been constant sources of information. In addition to the preceding, Francis Waring Robinson of the Detroit Institute of Arts must be named as my mentor and friend who guided me in my early museum career.

I am indebted more than I can acknowledge to the advice, help, and continued support of Emily Teeter, at the Oriental Institute Museum, University of Chicago. Her guidance, friendly criticism, and friendship have been invaluable to me at almost every stage in the preparation of this work. In addition, W. Benson Harer, M.D., and Sandra Knudsen, formerly a curator at the Toledo Museum of Art, commented on some part of the text, for which I thank them. Many discussions with Elsie Holmes Peck, my wife, have added greatly to the substance of this work. Considerable credit and thanks must go to Beatrice Rehl, Sarah McColl, Anastasia Graf, Camilla Knapp, and the other members of the staff at Cambridge University Press who have made this book possible. Opinions, errors, or omissions are my responsibility alone.

My thanks to the following individuals and institutions: The Metropolitan Museum of Art through the agency of Art Resource, Eileen Sullivan; Kristen Wenger of the British Museum; Ruth Bowler of the Walters Art Museum; and Robert Hensleigh of the Detroit Institute of Arts, for providing a number of illustrations. James Allen kindly supplied one image and Duane Stapp provided some of the drawings, for which I thank them. Other drawings and images were supplied by the author.

Introduction

Concerning Egypt there is no other country that possesses so many wonders.

HERODOTUS

For many people today any mention of Egypt brings to mind images of pyramids and mummies, the products of an ancient and mysterious civilization so old as to defy imagination. The modern fascination with ancient Egypt and its monuments is seemingly without end and never seems to be satisfied. The land of Egypt and its culture provide the material for countless films, special presentations on television, and sensational news articles about recent excavations. Every new archaeological discovery is hailed as "the greatest find since King Tut." So many misconceptions and misunderstandings abound concerning the history and archaeology of Egypt that it is often difficult to separate simple fact from romantic fiction. However, it is still possible even after so many centuries to know a great deal about how the Egyptians really lived, how they conducted their affairs, and the kinds of objects and materials they used.

The allure of the great monuments and the secrets of mummification cannot take away from the obvious fact that these ancient peoples were human beings. They lived their lives in a culture that seems foreign in many ways to us today, but they had many of the same basic needs that we do. Certainly there are differences in the ways many things were done, but this is more a matter of the long progress of developing technology rather than differences in culture. It is always amazing to see how many of the ordinary aspects of life have not changed from the way that the Egyptians carried them out thousands of years ago. We have excellent evidence of many aspects of their life to prove this, from the dwellings they lived in and the clothes they wore to the food they ate and even the games they played.

There have been many books written about the "daily life" of the ancient Egyptians in efforts to explain the various aspects of their culture. These works usually go far beyond examining how people

FIGURE 1   **Fishing and fowling. Dynasty Eighteen**
Facsimile of a painting from Theban Tomb 52, tomb of Nakht
This famous tomb painting is best known for the scene of hunting and fishing shown in the upper section. However, the lower register contains depictions of great interest as well. These include the harvesting of grapes, processing of wine, trapping of ducks and geese, preparation of the fowl, and the presentation of fish, fowl, and fruit to add to the piles of produce before the deceased and his wife.
Norman de Garis Davies (1865–1941), the Metropolitan Museum of Art, Rogers Fund, 1915 (15.5.19e). Reproduction of any kind is prohibited without express written permission in advance from the Metropolitan Museum of Art.

lived and the materials they used and include attempts to explain in detail the lengthy history, complex religion, and strangely different artistic styles. So much is known about this ancient civilization from the work of modern scholars that it is hardly needed to repeat the same kinds of information found in the popular books available on topics such as the technical aspects of mummification or the construction methods used to create the justly famous architecture. What might be more useful to the general reader or the student is the discussion here of the culture of the ancient Egyptians from the standpoint of the basic materials that were employed to make life possible and perhaps even enjoyable.

One of the misconceptions about ancient Egypt that should be addressed from the beginning is the mistaken idea that customs and processes never changed. The simple fact is that over the three thousand years of history of the ancient culture many things changed, and the differences can be identified and documented. We are able to see that the Egyptians were conscious of ideas of style and adaptable to new technologies, and we can produce abundant evidence to prove this. When a question is raised about any aspect of the culture, the answer must be qualified within a time frame. The life and technologies of 2500 BCE were not the same as those in 1230 BCE. As it was in almost every culture aspects of Egyptian life evolved so that a description of clothing or pottery or furniture at any one time would not necessarily apply to the same materials in another period. The Egypt of Cleopatra was distant from the time of the Pyramids by twenty-five hundred years, and the cultural and material changes in that time reflected the distance.

Over its long history Egyptian civilization became highly developed in many areas of the arts and crafts. The questions that are usually asked in the investigation of the material aspects of any culture and people, past or present, have to do with their dwellings, costume, objects of daily use, food and drink, tools for various occupations, methods of transport, and methods of production. How all of these originated and developed can be traced with the many clues that are available to us. It is possible to reconstruct the picture of these aspects of the life of the ancient Egyptians from the wealth of archaeological artifacts that have been preserved. The great number of objects that have come down to us provide many concrete examples of the kinds of things made, used, and sometimes treasured.

Basically there are three categories of information that contribute to our knowledge. They include the actual preserved objects, which are certainly the most direct evidence; the artistic representations in temples and tombs, which add a great deal; and the written descriptions in texts, which add still more information. All of these together inform us about the details of the material culture. However, caution has to be applied to all of this evidence. The life illustrated in the tombs and many of the objects preserved in them is that of the noble, elite, or privileged classes in ancient Egypt. To use these as a standard of how everyone lived probably gives a seriously distorted view. We have far less evidence concerning the common people and how they managed their lives and occupations, and it would obviously be incorrect to assume that their life was completely similar to the life of the nobility.

A remarkable asset for the study of the life of the ancient Egyptians is the abundant amount of information available in the form of preserved objects. No other ancient civilization has provided us with the extensive opportunity to experience so much of the material culture of antiquity as has ancient Egypt. The dry climate contributed to the natural preservation of many types of perishable objects, including papyrus documents, wooden furniture, clothing and other articles of textile, sandals of leather, and even fans made of feathers. The traditional religious belief of providing material goods in the tomb for the life of the spirit after death caused the Egyptians to leave behind a wide range of possessions that were needed, used, and even treasured. As a result we are able to see firsthand what was used, imagine how it was employed, and investigate the details of how it was made. A catalog of such objects includes a range of items from clothing and personal ornament, such as jewelry, to tools, weapons, and playthings, creating a virtual encyclopedia of ancient life as it was lived on the banks of the Nile.

In addition to the actual objects, the religious custom of depicting detailed views of activities on the walls of tombs makes it possible to supplement the objects with illustrations of many of the trades and crafts. It is often possible to examine all of the important steps in a process of manufacture. There are many instances of this, but a typical example will illustrate how complete the documentation can be. The production of bread begins with the growing of cereal crops and ends with the finished staple food. Paintings or relief carvings on tomb walls depict the process of plowing and sowing seed, the types of animals used to pull the plow, and the construction of the tools employed. Actual examples of plows have also been found. The sowing of the grain is presented, and the types of bags for transporting and storing the seed are preserved. The harvesting or cutting of the grain is illustrated, and examples of the wooden sickles with cutting edges made from flint blades have been found. The actions of threshing to separate the grain from the straw and the winnowing to remove the chaff are carved and painted in detail on tomb walls. Wooden paddles or scoops used to throw the grain into the air in the winnowing process have also been discovered. Even more evidence is provided by small models made to be put into the tomb for the benefit of the spirit, where the grinding of the grain to make flour is depicted and the bakery organization of both bread production and the brewing of beer are detailed in three dimensions. These activities will be discussed at greater length in the chapter on food and drink.

A third class of information is preserved in the form of documentary evidence with the actual objects and the artistic representations of how they were used. These "documents" can be as simple as a short notation on a broken piece of pottery or as complex as a lengthy list detailing the contents of a temple storeroom or the food rations for a workforce. This kind of evidence includes a wide range of examples extending from temple inventories to personal laundry lists. Contracts with tradesmen for the making of furniture and other household objects or the lists of the provisions allotted to crews of workmen all add to our knowledge of what was used and valued, how it was traded, or how it was obtained.

There are many things about the material world of ancient Egypt that will never be known, but the amount of information we have on some aspects of life among the Egyptians is so vast that we have the unusual chance to investigate and understand it as nowhere else among ancient cultures. The Egyptians seemed to be very literal-minded in one respect: the belief in an afterlife was such that you could "take it with you" – if you could afford it. The affluent could furnish their tombs with their possessions and paraphernalia of this life to be used in the next world. This custom does result in another very important misconception that is often held about ancient Egypt. A general misunderstanding about the Egyptians is that they were obsessed with ideas of death; one has only to study the complex process of mummification as it developed over the centuries to make this assumption. In fact, the Egyptians seemed to be in love with life and wanted more than anything else to prepare for a "goodly burial" that would insure a continuation of life in the next world. This elaborate preparation with the provision of material goods almost guaranteed that archaeologists and historians would be able to study the various aspects of crafts and technologies in great detail from preserved objects.

As artifacts have been discovered and studied from the successive dynasties in the long history of Egypt it seems possible to infer information about developing technologies from the advanced quality and expanding quantity of the material preserved. A typical example to support this assumption is illustrated by the kinds of objects that have been found that originated in the time before the beginning of writing and before Egypt was unified under one rule. Called the Predynastic Period, this was an era when settlements along the banks of the Nile had first begun to become more complex and better organized, a period considered to be the beginnings of urbanization, the move to living in villages and towns. The evolution of types of pottery, stone vessels, cosmetics palettes, tools, and weapons during the Predynastic Period tends to support ideas of a progressing civilization where the crafts and trades were becoming the occupations of highly specialized workmen.

What does this specialization mean for the craftsmen and their families? In a culture with developed craft production it is almost certain that the craftsmen no longer had to provide directly for their own food and other daily needs. They are no longer the hunters or the farmers, but they exchange their time, skills, and experience with those who are. The skillfully made pottery of the Predynastic Period clearly shows a high level of tradition, experience, and craftsmanship. The vessels made from hard stone of varied colors also suggest a degree of technical skill and artistic sensitivity that is almost hard to imagine in a culture where the formulation of a written language is only just beginning to develop. It seems logical to deduce that specialization of labor, where skills are learned and practiced in agreement with others who learn and practice other trades, was one of the steps on the way to a more complex society. Thus, the material finds shed light on human activity, even in a period when there are no written records to turn to.

It is also easy to move to conclusions that are not completely supported by the information available. Perhaps one could propose that some of the emerging ideas about crafts or technology may have been brought from some outside source because they seem to appear suddenly in a culture. This may or may not be the case, and this is an example where care must be taken in making assumptions, particularly about the formative period before the appearance of written evidence. It is always important when studying ancient Egypt, or any other ancient culture, to remember that the evidence may not be complete and interpretations may be subject to change in the light of new discoveries. There are a number of factors that cause this. Material from the south in Egypt and from dry tombs vastly outweighs the finds from the north, where fragile objects were not as often preserved in the wet conditions of the Nile delta. Objects that might have otherwise provided valuable information may have simply disappeared due to decay or vandalism

There are also clear gaps in the different kinds of records that have come down to us. The regular annual flooding of the Nile, so vital to the development of agriculture, washed away or buried evidence that would have been useful to complete the archaeological picture. Our imaginary picture of ancient Egyptian life is also slanted because of a preferred use of some materials. Temples and tombs were the structures considered most important for religious reasons and were built of seemingly durable stone; they were intended to last for eternity. The dwellings for the living, rich and poor, royal and common, were made of perishable unbaked mud brick that often did not survive as well. In short, all evidence of the material world of the ancient Egyptians must be studied with care and with due regard for the geography, physical conditions, context where it was found, and even techniques used by the archaeologists who found it.

The amazing range of preserved artifacts has been a fascinating study from the beginnings of modern interest in ancient Egypt. As the country became more receptive to foreign visitors and scholars in the nineteenth and twentieth centuries, objects and artifacts were collected for their value not only as curiosities but also for what they could reveal about the ancient civilization. Clothing, furniture, tools, weapons, cosmetic articles, and other useful objects have provided the details of history that would otherwise have been unknown. It may seem obvious but, with few exceptions, the texts of ancient historians give us more information about statecraft and warfare than they do about the ordinary activities of life.

Additional caution is required in the interpretation of the preserved artifacts and the supplementary information of the graphic illustrations in the tombs. It would be simple to make the assumption that, because some chairs and beds have been preserved, everyone in Egyptian society had the luxury of wooden furniture, something we might take for granted today. This is not necessarily true and will be a subject for examination later. There is also an inclination to simplify the discussion or description of types of artifacts, assuming that they were typical or standard. In actuality, styles and uses changed over the long history of Egypt. From the information we have, the clothing styles and design of the Old Kingdom seem remarkably different from that of the New Kingdom, roughly a millennium later. Egypt was certainly not an unchanging society, and this has to be taken into account in any discussion of the life of the people and the materials they used.

In the modern mind there is a strong tendency to make the general assumption that there was little change in the ancient world – that the lives of the Egyptians, Assyrians, Greeks, or Romans were pretty much the same throughout their respective histories. As it is usually described in history texts, the period termed Pharaonic Egypt – the time of the Pharaohs – lasted more than three thousand years. Although the history of the Greek and Roman world did not last as long in comparison to Egypt, there was development and change in those cultures in almost every aspect of life. It would be hard to imagine that there was little or no change in ancient

Egypt if one only considers how quickly styles are replaced and fads come and go today. The ancient peoples were no less inventive and interested in new ideas. The alterations and adjustments may not have been so radical or obvious to us, but any study of art and customs will make it clear that there were remarkable advances in many aspects of how life was lived, even in a society as rigidly structured as Egypt. In Egypt innovation and change were certainly constrained by attention to honored tradition and customary usage, but nevertheless change, however gradual, still occurred. It is those changes that make a study of the material world of ancient Egypt more complex, more multifaceted, and in many ways more interesting.

Geography and Geology: The Land

1

Generally speaking, we may say that the Nile surpasses all the rivers of the
inhabited world in its benefactions to mankind.

DIODORUS SICULUS

"The land of Egypt is the gift of the river," one of the most often quoted observations about ancient Egypt, was made by Herodotus, the fifth-century BCE Greek historian. It was not an original idea of his, and he may have even borrowed it from another ancient author, but it was a common way in his time to describe the dependence that the country had on the life-giving renewal brought by the annual inundation, or flooding, of the river Nile. His statement also emphasized the fact that the fertile Nile delta had been built up over centuries by the silt carried downstream each year by that flood, and it was fundamentally the delta that the world of the Greeks and Romans knew best.

The landscape of Egypt as seen from space has been compared to a lotus flower on a long stalk, with only one large leaf on one side. In a satellite image the long ribbon of the Nile and the narrow cultivated area along its banks terminates in the fan-shaped delta, the "flower." The "leaf" is the Fayum depression on the west, with its large lake. Although it is obviously a coincidence, the visual comparison of Egypt to the lotus is an apt one because the ancient Egyptians had a strong belief in the symbolism of the flower as an image of rebirth or resurrection.

One of the most remarkable aspects of the Egyptian landscape is the sharp division that can be seen between the sand of the desert and the rich black land of the cultivated areas (Fig. 2). The two are in such sharp contrast that it is possible to stand with one foot in the desert and the other on soil where crops are growing. In antiquity the Egyptians called the cultivated land, the black earth, *kemit* and the desert, with its red sand, *deshret*. They termed themselves "the people of the black land."

On maps with the usual modern orientation, with north at the top, the area traditionally termed Lower Egypt is the land from the

FIGURE 2   The Nile valley at Saqqara
The clear demarcation between the desert and the cultivation can be seen
in the lower part of the image. The mountain range in the east of the valley is
in the far distance. In the region of Memphis the Nile valley begins to widen into
the fan-shaped delta.
Author's photograph

area of modern Cairo north to the Mediterranean Sea. Upper Egypt
is at the bottom of the modern map. "Upper Egypt" is upriver;
"Lower Egypt" is downriver (Fig. 3). This is usually confusing to
people with a preconceived "north is upper because it is at the top"
orientation, but it made perfect sense to the Egyptians. Throughout
Egyptian history the unity of the country was expressed in the
phrase "the two lands," acknowledging the contrast between the
lush lands of the delta and the arid desert-mountain landscape of the
country farther south. In the past it was assumed that the reverent
use of the term "the two lands" was a memory of the time before
the country was unified, but now it is assumed to refer to the eternal unity of the two distinct parts of the country, Upper and Lower
Egypt, as one entity, and it emphasizes their character as particular
parts of the whole.

Throughout its history ancient Egypt was basically an agricultural country with a rural, farming-based economy (Fig. 4). This
is well demonstrated by both the archaeological remains and the
many preserved painted and carved representations of the work in
the fields and on the estates. A traveler in Egypt today might be
impressed by the rice fields in the Nile delta and the sugarcane fields

FIGURE 3   The Nile in the region of Beni Hassan, in Middle Egypt
            Little cultivation separates the bank of the river from the hills in the
            east in this area. The narrow farmland is bound in by the desert in
            the west and the rising hills in the east.
            Author's photograph

in the south, especially around modern Luxor. The cotton grown in
Egypt has also become famous for its character and quality. These
three crops, rice, sugarcane, and cotton, were not known to the
ancient Egyptians and were not historically part of their essential
produce. Potatoes, native to the New World, were also unknown.
However, the Egyptians had a diet of considerable variety, with
access to a range of vegetables, fruits, and grains, as well as animal
and fish products. They kept bees for honey and cultivated grapes
to produce wine. Food and drink are prominently mentioned in the
standard prayers for the well-being of the departed as "bread and
beer, and all good things."

The land of Egypt was rich in one raw material that had a tremen-
dous influence on the culture, and that was an abundance of different
types of stone. Unlike the ancient civilizations of Mesopotamia, for
whom stone was comparatively rare and often had to be imported
from a far distance, the ancient Egyptians had access to a variety
of types of stone, which made many kinds of construction possible.

FIGURE 4   A cultivated area in the narrow fertile land along the Nile
No longer renewed by the annual flood since the rising of the Aswan dam, the
cultivated areas are still rich and productive from the use of fertilizer.
Author's photograph

Stone was used freely for buildings, for carved sculpture, as tools, and
for personal decoration, as well as a source of mineral raw materials.

The bedrock of the country is made up of sedimentary rocks,
which rest on metamorphic and igneous rock. These latter rocks are
most visible where they are exposed in the south, in the region of
Aswan and the First Cataract of the Nile. The granites and grano-
diorites of Aswan were the source for much of the hard stone used
for sculpture, obelisks, and temple fixtures such as doorways, altars,
and shrines.

The next important stone resource is termed Nubian sandstone,
exposed to a great extent in the south of Egypt and the northern Sudan. This sandstone was the principal building material for
Egyptian temples from the time of the New Kingdom. Because of
its great tensile strength, it was suitable for the construction of the
larger and more impressive examples of temple architecture we commonly associate with ancient Egypt. Nubian (Egyptian) sandstone is
usually a golden brown from the presence of iron oxide. Above the
sandstone in more northern parts of Egypt is a layer of limestone

FIGURE 5   **The rock-cut tombs of the Middle Kingdom at Beni Hassan**
The mountain range in the east in this region of Egypt provided a
natural location for the cutting of local tombs.
Author's photograph

and shale. The royal and private tombs in the Theban area (at modern Luxor) are carved into these limestone hills, and some types of
limestone were often used for special building purposes because of
their near-white color and compact quality. Both the sandstone and
limestone layers are sedimentary rock that formed when the region
was submerged beneath a shallow sea (Fig. 5).

There are a number of other kinds of stone found in Egypt,
including quartzite, hematite, Egyptian alabaster (calcite, sometimes
termed travertine), and porphyry, but the major architectural stones
were granite, sandstone, and limestone. Other types of stone were
chosen for their color, special markings, hardness, or adaptability for
certain types of sculpture. As just one special example, turquoise was
mined from early times in the Sinai Peninsula for its color and was
used extensively in jewelry making.

The single most important physical asset in ancient Egypt was the
river Nile, which served not only as a water supply and a source of
annual renewal of the farmland but also as the main means of transportation. The Nile was fed by the summer rains in the mountains

of east Africa. The water of the river could be seen to increase in southern Egypt around the first of May. It continued to rise until around the first of September, when it reached its maximum height, and it began to subside in October. The river rose as much as ten meters (more than thirty feet) in the south of Egypt and as much as eight meters (more than twenty-four feet) at Memphis, in the region of modern Cairo. With this annual flooding came a fresh supply of river silt, or fine mud, which served to renew the agricultural land.

Since the amount of flooding was dependent on the summer rains, any appreciable variation in the quantity of rain could have disastrous consequences for Egypt. Too high an inundation caused flooding that sometimes wiped out whole settlements and towns; too little resulted in a shortage of food and consequent famine. Early in history the Egyptians developed methods of measuring the flood by making observations in the south and predicting the results for the north. Water was the lifeblood of ancient Egypt – without it there was only disaster.

The agricultural cycle was naturally dictated by the rising of the Nile. When the waters had sufficiently subsided, the boundary markers were reestablished and the fields were easily plowed for the winter sowing of the new crops of barley, emmer wheat, and flax. The rich new layer of silt and the residual damp earth made for a flourishing agricultural economy, but much depended on the reliability of the annual flood. From necessity the Egyptians developed additional methods of irrigation to supplement the waters of the inundation. They learned to trap some of the floodwater in pools with small dams and levees and gradually let it out into the fields. Depictions of workers carrying buckets of water suspended from a yoke across their backs show them taking it from the Nile in order to water farm plots.

It was probably in the late New Kingdom that a more elaborate device was invented that is still in limited use in some places today. This was the shaduf, a lever with a bucket attached to a rope on one end and a counterweight on the other. With several of these on stepped terraces of the river bank, water could be lifted from the surface of the river to fields at a considerable height above. The sakieh, a waterwheel driven by animal power, was not introduced into Egypt until the time of the Greeks and Romans. In classical times the shaduf and the sakieh were supplemented by the Archimedes screw, a large tube with an interior screw that could raise water as it was turned. All three of these devices were still widely used in the twentieth century, but they are gradually being supplanted and replaced by gasoline and electric pumps.

FIGURE 6   Elephantine Island at Aswan
The First Cataract of the Nile at Aswan with the rock outcroppings
defines and restricts the width of the river and at one time marked
the southern boundary of the country.
Author's photograph

With the raising of the present dam at Aswan in the 1960s the cycle of the inundation, as it had been known since antiquity, could no longer continue. Water is retained at the dam and can be released as needed. One of the great benefits of the dam is that electric power has become available to almost everyone. The negative side of this modern development is that the renewal of the land with silt from the south is no longer possible. In the past the annual flood also served to remove some of the ground salts, but this also no longer happens. The huge lake behind the dam has also served to change the climate of Upper Egypt so that the annual rainfall has increased in a land where many buildings are still made of unbaked mud brick, thus causing important changes in building maintenance and construction.

The geography of ancient Egypt had a definite restrictive character, in that the mountains and deserts, the Mediterranean Sea in the north, and the cataracts, the narrow gorges cut through areas of hard stone in the south, acted as protective barriers for the Nile valley and its inhabitants (Fig. 6). Over the centuries this geographical semi-isolation influenced the worldview of the Egyptians and was a major contributing factor to the long life of the civilization. However, the Egyptians were never without some degree of contact with Western Asia across the Sinai Peninsula and with lands to the south beyond the cataracts. In addition, expeditions were regularly sent by sea to the west coast of Asia and to the east coast of Africa in the south. Trading missions to lands outside the valley of the Nile began early in the first dynasties. Raw materials that were not available or plentiful in Egypt were imported, sometimes from great distances. Cedar from the Lebanon forests; lapis lazuli blue stone from sources as far away as Afghanistan; and ivory, ebony, gold, and even incense-bearing trees from farther south in Africa, were among the resources acquired by trade or conquest. The material world of the ancient Egyptians could be rich and varied, as is reflected in the use of exotic materials and rich decoration in the arts and crafts. Lifestyles were limited by geography, but the imaginative use of local assets – from the mud of the Nile turned into pottery and brick to the wealth of stones employed in architecture and art – testifies to the ingenuity and skills developed over the course of Pharaonic history.

Baines, J., and J. Málek. *Atlas of Ancient Egypt*. New York: Facts on File, 1980.

Butzer, K. W. *Early Hydraulic Civilization in Egypt*. Chicago: University of Chicago Press, 1976.

James, T. G. H. *The British Museum Concise Introduction to Ancient Egypt*. Ann Arbor: University of Michigan Press, 2005.

An Introduction to Ancient Egypt. London: British Museum, 1979.

Kees, H. *Ancient Egypt: A Cultural Topography*. Chicago: University of Chicago Press, 1961.

Sampsell, B. M. *A Traveler's Guide to the Geology of Egypt*. Cairo: American University in Cairo Press, 2003.

Brief Outline of Egyptian History

2

What is proudly advertised as Egyptian history is merely a collection of rags and tatters.

SIR ALAN GARDINER

PREDYNASTIC PERIOD – CIRCA 5300–3000 BCE

Areas of North Africa along the south coast of the Mediterranean Sea began to become attractive for settlement after the end of the last Ice Age (around 10,000 BCE), especially where there was an available supply of fresh water. The Nile River and the small but fertile areas around its banks were particularly appealing to the peoples who were just beginning to emerge from a nomadic lifestyle and starting to seek hospitable locations in which to settle. From 10,000 to about 5000 BCE there is little preserved evidence of advancement in lifestyles from those of the Late Paleolithic (Old Stone Age). The evidence for these first dwellers in the Nile valley consists mainly of stone tools of types recognized in other parts of the world during the prehistoric period, primarily implements developed for chopping, pounding, and scraping. There is only some scattered evidence of art as it is known in other areas of the prehistoric world. There is a small number of examples of images and designs scratched on the rock outcroppings in desert areas, but there are also petroglyphs preserved in the Nile valley itself.

The beginnings of more advanced cultural directions can be documented by physical evidence during the period between roughly 5000 and 4500 BCE. This is the start of an age that Egyptologists term the Predynastic Period, literally the time before the recorded dynasties (groups of hereditary rulers). The approximately fifteen hundred years (4500 to around 3000 BCE) that make up the last phase of the Predynastic Period were a time of rapid change and development. The practices of agriculture, including the cultivation of emmer wheat, barley, and flax, and the domestication of animals, especially sheep, goats, and pigs, became central to life as villages and towns expanded and were organized to accommodate larger groups of people who chose to live together for mutual aid and protection. The rapid advancement in agriculture implies that the early dwellers also began to design and use more complex tools in the process.

The time from 4500 to around 3000 BCE was also the formative period of Egyptian civilization when the basic elements of its culture were developed. Art and crafts began to progress and become formalized, and the beginning of the fourth millennium BCE saw the emergence of specialized craftsmen who provided services to an emerging consumership. A written language had its beginnings for record keeping, and the Egyptian principal of kingship (a supreme ruler sanctioned by the gods) made its appearance. Geographical and societal allegiances were formed and local leadership in towns and villages emerged. Domestic architecture was based largely on the use of available growth of plants and reeds.

Not all parts of the country developed at the same rate during this time, and Upper Egypt seems to have been in the lead in the creation of large population centers and in the process of social specialization, but recent excavations in the Nile delta appear to indicate that the north was not so far behind in its development as was once thought.

Around 3000 BCE a remarkable change was made in the makeup of the country when it was gradually unified and brought together under the control of one ruler. It is thought that the more advanced or better organized leaders of Middle and Upper Egypt in the south conquered the less well-prepared dwellers in Lower Egypt in the north (mainly the Nile delta). On the *Narmer Palette*, a two-sided relief carving, one such victory of the south over the north is illustrated. This artifact was long considered the actual record of the unification of the country, but it is now thought that it might represent only one of several events rather that the single one that brought the two parts of the land together.

Contact and trade with other areas of the ancient world outside of Egypt are attested during the Predynastic Period. In the past the development of writing was assumed to have been inspired, if not directly influenced, by exchange with the cultures of Mesopotamia to the east. It is more probable that the separate systems of writing evolved independently to meet similar needs in rising cultures. Useful crafts, including pottery making and stone working, reached a high level of accomplishment in Egypt during this early period.

From burials of the time it can be inferred that there was already belief in a life after death that had to be provided for with material goods. Personal objects such as pottery and stone tools were included in the grave, presumably for use of the spirit in the afterlife. These include not only containers for food offerings but flint knives and stone palettes for the preparation of cosmetics. The body was usually placed in its grave in a contracted position and mainly, but not always, facing to the west, to the setting sun, suggesting that the belief in an afterlife also included a destination for the spirit in the west, the land of the dead. It is clear that many of the basic rudiments of ancient Egyptian civilization were already present in this time before writing and before history.

EARLY DYNASTIC PERIOD, DYNASTIES ONE AND TWO – CIRCA 3000–2686 BCE

The history of Egypt is divided by scholars into three large time periods that are termed the Old, Middle, and New Kingdoms. These three eras of strong cultural identity are the main epochs in which the Egyptians reached the highest levels of their accomplishment. Egyptian history is further divided into thirty-one dynasties (families or related hereditary rulers) following the work of an Egyptian priest-historian named Manetho who lived in the third century BCE. Unfortunately, Manetho's history has not been wholly preserved and we have to rely on excerpts and quotations found in other ancient authors, but the general structure is relatively clear. The reason for the change from one dynasty to the next is not always obvious and some dynasties coexisted, but generally the members of the dynasties of Egypt were united by blood. The framework provided by Manetho, even with its problems of overlaps of some rulers and the omission of others, is still the best general outline of the royal succession. The Early Dynastic Period (Dynasties One and Two) is followed by the Old Kingdom (Dynasties Three through Six). Modern scholars have also inserted a Dynasty Zero, acknowledging that there were some early rulers who are not recorded in Manetho's Dynasty One.

The Early Dynastic Period was a time of great advancement in the organization of the state and society, the development of writing, and the attention paid to burial, particularly the burial of the early kings. According to the Egyptians' own traditions a king named Menes was honored as the founder of the country and as the ruler who established the city of Memphis at the apex of the Nile delta as the capital. In addition to the then recently founded city of Memphis, south of the site of modern Cairo, Abydos in Upper

Egypt was an important center at the time. Hierakonpolis in Upper Egypt and Buto in the delta were among the sites the Egyptians considered of great antiquity, but current explorations have added to our ideas about the state of civilization in the delta at the time. The burials of the early kings in large tombs in the desert at Abydos attest to its early importance to the rulers of Upper Egypt. At Saqqara, to the west of Memphis, many early royal officials were buried, and for some time there was scholarly argument about whether the kings of the early dynasties were also buried there.

The remains in the tombs of kings and officials of Dynasties One and Two demonstrate the development of craftsmanship, particularly in the production of beautifully worked stone vessels and objects in copper that were included among the grave goods for the employment of the spirit. The use of exotic, nonnative woods and other materials, including cedar, ebony, and ivory, also demonstrates that trade was developing at this early date between Egypt and the Lebanon to the east as well as from the south in Africa.

In Dynasty Two there is evidence of internal strife and a struggle to identify one of two prominent gods, Horus or Seth, as a pre-eminent deity and patron of kingship. This seems to have been resolved by a king named Khasekhemwy, whose name means "the two powers have risen." The first royal portrait statues that have been preserved are from this time. Advancements were being made in technology as evidenced by the developments in sculpture as well as in the use of stone in architectural construction instead of the traditional mud brick.

OLD KINGDOM, DYNASTIES THREE THROUGH SIX – 2686–2160 BCE

In Dynasty Three important changes took place that initiate the beginning of the first great period in Egyptian history. With Dynasty Three there were rapid strides made in funerary architecture under its second king, Djoser (sometimes spelled Zoser). His Step Pyramid was the first large stone building of size in the world. It was an innovative and experimental structure because it obviously went through several changes of design. At first it was meant to be a mastaba tomb, along the lines of the tombs of the kings of Dynasties One and Two. Termed "mastaba" after its resemblance to a mud brick bench, the mastaba tomb had a rectangular superstructure with slightly tapering sides. The original shape was gradually expanded and layers were added to give it its final form, with superimposed and gradually smaller steps.

The important technological advance in the building of the Step Pyramid was the use of stone blocks instead of the more usual sun-dried mud brick normally employed in the construction of a tomb. These innovations of design and material are traditionally credited to Imhotep, vizier (chancellor) of Djoser, who in later times came to be revered as a great sage and architect. The structures in the complex around the Step Pyramid add to our knowledge about the state of religious ritual in Dynasty Three. These include the emerging importance of the cult of the sun, symbolized by the pyramid structure itself. Parts of the complex were designed for the festival ritual in which the king was symbolically rejuvenated, and other parts were meant to honor select gods of both Upper and Lower Egypt. The growing importance of the sun god in the Egyptian pantheon had begun to emerge as early as Dynasty Two, evidenced by a royal name, "Neb-Re," that was compounded with the name of the god. This development in Egyptian religion is signaled by more frequent appearances of the name of Re on other inscriptions from Heliopolis, to the east of Memphis.

Images of kingship evolved during the reign of Djoser. In a statue found in part of his Step Pyramid complex he is depicted as a strong, almost superhuman individual wearing the *nemes* headdress, an attribute of kingship that later became a permanent symbol of royalty. In relief carvings in the subterranean chambers of the pyramid and the nearby South Tomb he is shown in the act of the ceremonial race he ran as a part of his festival of renewal or rejuvenation. The chambers and adjacent halls were decorated with blue and blue-green tiles of Egyptian faience that by their number in the thousands testify to a capacity for organized production of the material on a large scale.

Nonroyal art also made advances in Dynasty Three, as evidenced by the decoration of private tombs of the period. Cultural and artistic accomplishments mirrored the advances made in the social and political areas. Large building projects such as Djoser's pyramid complex reflect the existence of an organized state with access to resources of materials, a large labor force, and specialized artists/craftsmen.

Senefru, the first king of Dynasty Four, is thought to have finished the pyramid that is partly preserved at the site of Meidum, south of Saqqara, the necropolis of Memphis. For reasons that are not known, Senefru moved north to Dashur, where he completed two others, called in modern times the Bent Pyramid and the Red

Pyramid. Following Senefru's innovations Dynasty Four was to become the great age of the pyramid builders. What was begun with the Step Pyramid of Djoser was brought to its highest stage of development under Khufu and his successors, Khafre and Menkaure. These three rulers are also known by the Greek translations of their names – Cheops, Chephren, and Mycerinus – but the more acceptable usage is the Egyptian form of the names.

Advancements had been made in every field – statecraft, trade, agriculture, engineering, mathematics, medicine, and, to cite the most visible and enduring example, construction in stone. Technical skills, including the mastery of mathematics and geometry, are evident in the precision with which the monuments were constructed. The evidence provided by the size and architectural perfection of the Egyptian pyramids is a graphic reminder of the development of a complex society and a growing bureaucracy.

Khufu succeeded his father, Senefru, and embarked on one of the largest building projects ever undertaken. The Great Pyramid of Giza, designed to be the eternal resting place of the king and a visual expression of the reverence for the sun god, surpassed any construction envisioned before. In its finished state it rose 480 feet high, covered thirteen acres, and utilized about two and a half million limestone blocks. This structure provides us with several kinds of information about the state of Egyptian society. The king was "the living Horus," the manifestation of that god on earth and the conduit through which mankind could come into contact with the gods. It was thought essential that his tomb exceed anything even dreamed of before. Beyond the religious significance, it is important to consider the infrastructure needed to support such an activity as pyramid building: the army of workmen who cut stone in the quarries, both at the limestone plateau of Giza and at the Tura quarries across the river to the east; the corps of men who transported the stone on sledge and barge; and the "support troops" who provided the food and drink for the workmen; to say nothing of the skilled architects and managers who were responsible for design and orientation, logistics, and construction control. The picture that emerges is one of a very complicated bureaucracy, controlled by an aristocracy mainly related to the royal house, as exemplified by princes Nefermaat and Hemiunu, who had titles like "Overseer of the Works of the King."

The arts flourished. The elaborate and detailed representations in private tombs bear witness to the specialized crafts where sculptors and jewelers, boatwrights and potters are shown at work on their crafts. The high level of a developing design sense for domestic use is shown, not only in tomb reliefs depicting furniture but in a few rare examples of actual royal furniture preserved, as well as in the elegant costumes and royal regalia evident in sculptural representations.

Curiously, there is little known about the personalities of the important rulers of Dynasty Four. Their monuments tell us virtually nothing about them. There is more information in the tomb inscriptions of the elite class. As in all periods Egyptian history has to be pieced together from many different sources.

In Dynasty Five the early kings constructed a pyramid complex at Abusir between Giza and Saqqara. In addition to pyramids for royal burial, shrines or temples to the sun god were built, attesting to the continued developing power of Re. These religious structures contained an open courtyard with an obelisk of massive but rather squat proportions. Foreign campaigns and the exploitation of distant resources continued to expand the influence of Egypt in the Near East. Depictions on the walls of the sun temples show images of foreign, nonnative animals such as bears imported as gifts for the king and the gods. Later kings of Dynasty Five included, for the first time, religious texts carved in the interior chambers of their pyramids, whereas earlier pyramids in Dynasty Four had no such decoration.

The tomb chambers of private persons of Dynasties Five and Six contain in their limited "biographies" references to the governmental activities for which they were responsible and thus add to knowledge about the affairs of the time. In Dynasty Six the strong central control from the capital at Memphis declined and regional rulers assumed more power in their local areas. The reason for the weakening of royal rule is not entirely clear. It has been suggested that serious climatic changes affected the economy, and the lengthy rule of progressively weaker kings may have added to or resulted in the erosion of royal power.

FIRST INTERMEDIATE PERIOD, DYNASTIES SEVEN THROUGH ELEVEN – 2160–2055 BCE

"Intermediate Period" is the term used for the transitional historical eras between the important and noteworthy periods in Egypt. Little is known about Dynasties Seven and Eight except that Dynasty Eight consisted of weak kings centered at Memphis. Dynasties Nine and Ten had their home at Herakleopolis, in Middle Egypt. They controlled the north while the south was under the rule of princes of Thebes in Upper Egypt (Dynasty Eleven in the south). The artistic traditions were carried on in the provinces but were not of the quality maintained by the royal workshops of Memphis in the Old Kingdom. However, the lack of centralized control in the arts provided provincial artists with opportunities for experimentation and a limited degree of innovation.

MIDDLE KINGDOM, DYNASTIES ELEVEN, TWELVE, AND THIRTEEN – 2055–1650 BCE

From the disunity of the First Intermediate Period a ruler of Thebes, Nebhetepre Mentuhotpe, reunited the country and made it once again politically and economically stable. Presumably the Herakleopolitans were defeated under his leadership, but little is known about the actual process. From about this time comes the remarkable group of tomb models made for a man named Meketre that illustrate in three dimensions many of the crafts that were earlier represented in the carving and painting on Old Kingdom tomb walls.

Dynasty Twelve, a new family of strong kings beginning with Amenemhet I, took control, and under their rule the country once again prospered (Fig. 7).

The royal residence was moved from Thebes to a site south of Memphis. Although they imitated their predecessors, the pyramid burial places of the Dynasty Twelve kings were not the solid stone of the Old Kingdom but mud brick construction built on a stone core with stone facing. This change in building practices implies not only a need for an economical use of labor but also a kind of innovation in combining different construction techniques to achieve the same results as their predecessors. The arts of painting, sculpture, and the crafts, especially jewelry making, flourished, not only in the royal capital but also in the provincial centers, particularly in Middle Egypt at Beni Hassan and El Bersha, and at Aswan in the south. The tombs of provincial rulers exhibit a wider range of subject matter and a leaning toward painted rather than carved walls in tombs. The subjects include depictions of battle and siege-craft, military training or athletic games, as well as records of the appearance in Egypt of foreign traders and craftsmen, all new to tomb decoration.

The reign of Senusret III, about halfway through Dynasty Twelve, marked an expansion of control into Nubia with the construction

FIGURE 7   The Bark Station or Chapel of King Senusret I at Karnak. Dynasty
                Twelve
                A reconstructed monument from the Middle Kingdom, this chapel
                is one of the rare examples of architecture preserved from this sec-
                ond period of prosperity in Egypt. It illustrates basic elements of
                Egyptian architecture: cubic design, out-curved cavetto cornice,
                and torus molding.
                Author's photograph

of a series of border forts. Recent excavations have added new information about expeditions to the land of Punt, on the Red Sea coast,
during this time. Trade with the areas to the south was especially
important for obtaining luxury goods such as gold, rare woods, and
exotic perfumes. In the art of the period, representations of the king
take on a new aspect, a "world-weary" appearance with lined faces and
deep sunken eyes, suggesting a conception of the ruler that is somehow more human than he had been depicted in the Old Kingdom.

Dynasty Thirteen lasted about 150 years and included a large
number of rulers who reigned for very short periods. The borders to
the south and to the east were no longer well protected and incursions by people from western Asia began to make a significant impact
on the country. Recent excavations at Tell el-Daba in the northeast
delta have shown that this site was occupied by foreigners by the end
of the dynasty. Dynasty Fourteen, which follows in Manetho's list,
was a group of weak kings who broke with the central control and
ruled in the eastern delta, and who were apparently contemporane-
ous with Dynasty Thirteen.

SECOND INTERMEDIATE PERIOD – 1650–1550 BCE

Matters came to a head in northern Egypt when the weak rulers in the eastern delta were replaced by foreign invaders who the Egyptians called *heqa khasut*, foreign rulers, or "rulers of hill countries." These were later known to Greek authors as Hyksos. The Hyksos comprised Dynasties Fifteen and Sixteen and ruled in the north for a little more than a hundred years. Native Egyptian rule continued in Thebes in the south with what Manetho in his history identified as Dynasty Seventeen. This new group of rulers eventually expelled the foreigners from the country.

An important consideration concerning the influx of foreign rulers and their people is the lasting effects this had on Egyptian civilization. Even though Egypt had had foreign contacts and trade from the Early Dynastic Period on, it was still a country to some extent isolated from outside influences. During the time of the Hyksos some new ideas were introduced. Among these were new and more effective techniques of metallurgy, new weaponry, and the use of the chariot. Until the Second Intermediate Period the wheel was rare in Egypt, in part due to the easy availability and traditional reliance on water transport.

NEW KINGDOM, DYNASTIES EIGHTEEN THROUGH TWENTY – 1550–1069 BCE

Seqenenre Tao and his son Kamose, the last kings of Dynasty Seventeen, fought to expel the Hyksos, but it was left to Ahmose, Kamose's brother, to finish the job and regain control of the country. Ahmose of Thebes was later revered as "the liberator," founded a new dynasty (Eighteen) and, with his son Amunhotep I, extended Egyptian control farther into Nubia in the south and into Palestine on the east. This was the beginning of one of the most prosperous periods in the history of Egypt. Amunhotep's successor, Thutmose I, extended Egyptian conquest in Asia to the Euphrates River and even farther to the south in Nubia.

Following the incursions of the Hyksos, Egypt was more open to a wider worldview. Ideas from outside the Nile valley would have effects on Dynasty Eighteen as it became a succession of kings named Amunhotep and Thutmose. These kings would capitalize on this wider outlook with not only the implementation of improved technologies but also more interest in the exploration and exploitation of foreign lands.

Thutmose II succeeded his father and married his half-sister Hatshepsut. When he died, his son, Thutmose III, followed him to the throne at a young age and Hatshepsut became the regent. Soon she assumed full control and had herself crowned king. The memorable events of her reign are commemorated in her funerary temple at Deir el Bahri, modeled on the precedent set by the nearby monument built by Nebhetepre Mentuhotpe, of Dynasty Eleven. These include the story of her divine conception by the god Amun, which legitimized her kingship, as well as accounts of her major exploits. These exceptional events in her reign include an expedition to the land of Punt on the east coast of Africa and the transport of the two obelisks for the Temple of Amun in Thebes. They are important for her history but they also stand as evidence to developments in trade and the crafts. The procurement of rare materials from a distant land and the technical accomplishments of quarrying and transporting huge monoliths are recorded in visual terms in order to memorialize the levels of her achievements.

It was traditional for historians to believe that Thutmose III began to erase the name and memory of Hatshepsut immediately after her demise. This is no longer thought true and in fact her images were not mutilated and her monuments usurped until well into his independent reign. He continued to occupy himself with military campaigns to secure Egypt's northern and southern borders as he had during Hatshepsut's regency. Foreign contacts and trade were expanded during his sovereignty and the prosperity of the country increased. During his long reign of more than fifty years he accomplished a number of important building projects, especially in the Temple of Amun at Karnak.

Amunhotep II carried on his father's military campaign with a renewed ferocity. His son, Thutmose IV, presided over a relatively peaceful period in Egypt, where diplomatic relations were extended and strengthened. As a result, his son, Amunhotep III, inherited a prosperous and stable kingdom in a country that had earned great respect and influence in the ancient world.

The reign of Amunhotep III was a flourishing period. He married a woman of nonroyal birth named Tiy and elevated her to the rank of chief wife. She was to have great influence not only on him and his policies but also on his son Amunhotep IV (who changed his name to Akhenaton). Complex diplomatic relations with the

FIGURE 8   **The Temple of Luxor. Dynasties Eighteen to Nineteen**
Built by Amunhotep III and added to by Ramesses II, the Luxor Temple is an example of architecture from the third great period in Egypt's history. The monumental construction of pylons and colonnades give evidence of the Egyptian mastery of building techniques in stone.
Author's photograph

kingdoms of western Asia are known through the chance preservation of a number of letters on clay now called the Amarna Tablets.

It was a great period of construction for Egypt. Amunhotep III further embellished the Temple of Amun at Karnak and created the major part of Luxor Temple (Fig. 8). On the west bank he built a royal palace and a large mortuary temple of which only the two mammoth statues, popularly known as the Colossi of Memnon, are the most visible evidence. Recent excavations at the site have revealed more of the plan and a considerable amount of the sculpture that decorated the temple. Amunhotep III was particularly active in the construction of temples in Nubia, the source of much of the wealth of the empire.

Amunhotep III's successor, Amunhotep IV, is better known today as Akhenaton, the name he assumed when he began to espouse the worship of a single solar deity called the Aton. With Akhenaton's single-minded attention to the sun as an image of god came an attempt at a social reorganization. The royal residence was moved from Thebes to the new city of Akhetaten, at a site in middle Egypt where a fresh start could begin, unhindered by old traditions. The city was laid out and organized around the open-air worship of the Aton. An unusual style was developed in the visual arts in which the king, his queen, Nefertiti, and their daughters were depicted in the rituals dedicated to the solar deity. Akhenaton's "revolution" lasted less than two decades, the residence then returned to Thebes, the city of Akhetaten was deserted, and the worship of the traditional pantheon of the Egyptian gods was restored.

Immediately following the time of Akhenaton's reign, usually termed the "Amarna Period" after the modern name of the site of his capital, came the reign of the most familiar name today, that of Tutankhamun. He was a minor king, died when still in his teens, and would be virtually forgotten except for the chance preservation of his tomb with its royal furnishings. The contents of the tomb are one of the best resources available for the study of the high level of Egyptian crafts of the New Kingdom, such as the making of jewelry, furniture, clothing, and even chariots.

After Tutankhamun an important general in his reign named Horemheb took the throne. He was followed by a new dynasty (Dynasty Nineteen), at first composed of strong military leaders. Of these kings Ramesses II is the best known, both for his military expeditions to the south in Africa and to the east into Syro-Palestine and for his widespread building projects throughout the Nile valley. Sometimes called "Ramesses the Great," he campaigned as far as the Euphrates River in Mesopotamia. He created the rock-cut temples to the south at Abu Simbel in Nubia, one of his most important and famous monuments (Fig. 9).

One of the last great rulers of Egypt was Ramesses III, of Dynasty Twenty. He was responsible for defending his country against invaders from Libya in the west and from the "Peoples of the Sea" in the eastern Nile delta. His mortuary temple on the west bank at Luxor is one of the better preserved temples of this period. The remainder of the dynasty saw a decrease in central rule, with the rise of power of the high priests at Thebes creating a separate kingly line.

THIRD INTERMEDIATE PERIOD – 1069–664 BCE

In Dynasty Twenty-One the rule of the country was once again divided. A royal line ruled from the western delta in competition with a group of high priests from Thebes in the south. Dynasty Twenty-Two was made up of kings of Libyan ancestry who, at times, attempted to reunify the country by bringing the south under

FIGURE 9   The rock-cut Temple of Ramesses II at Abu Simbel in Nubia. Dynasty Nineteen
The Abu Simbel temples are symbols of the expansion and domination of Nubia,
to the south. They also demonstrate the mastery of architects and designers who
envisioned the whole complex carved out of the mountainside.
Author's photograph

their control. At other times the rulers who are now identified as
belonging to Dynasties Twenty-One through Twenty-Four all
ruled simultaneously. Even though this was a tumultuous period in
Egyptian history, strong traditions in the arts and crafts were carried on. The techniques of metallurgy, especially, were developed.
The finds of royal burials at Tanis in the eastern Nile delta show
that skilled craftsmen were employed in the production of funerary
equipment and jewelry. Early in the eighth century BCE Kashta,
a ruler of Napata, in the south, made inroads to the north as far as
Aswan (and possibly as far north as Thebes), laying the groundwork
for Dynasty Twenty-Five.

LATE PERIOD – 664–332 BCE

Piankhy (Piye), the Napatan ruler who followed Kashta, occupied
the capital at Memphis in the north and began effective control of

the country. These peoples from the south considered themselves the legitimate inheritors of Egyptian rule and strove to revive ancient traditions and artistic usage. The seventh century saw a new prosperity, and the kings of Dynasty Twenty-Five engaged in building projects throughout Egypt, particularly in the Theban area. They were eventually ousted from the country by Assyrian invaders in 664 BCE. The Assyrians delegated control to princes of Sais in the delta, thus forming Dynasty Twenty-Six. This returned at least partial rule to native kings and fostered a revival of traditional artistic styles. Dynasty Twenty-Six is sometimes called the "Egyptian Renaissance" as a result.

Dynasty Twenty-Six lasted until the first invasion of Egypt by the Persians in 525 BCE. In 404 BCE rule returned to native Egyptians for a period that lasted less than fifty years (404–343 BCE) and included Dynasties Twenty-Eight through Thirty. The Persians invaded again in 343 and were finally ousted by Alexander the Great in 332.

PTOLEMAIC PERIOD – 332–30 BCE – AND ROMAN PERIOD – 30 BCE–395 CE

Alexander's conquest of Egypt and the Persian Empire and his later death left the country in the hands of Ptolemy Lagus, who founded his own Macedonian-Greek dynasty. This era is now known as the Ptolemaic Period (332–30 BCE). The Roman invasion of 30 BCE ended the rule of the famous queen Cleopatra VII, the last of the Ptolemaic line, when she was unsuccessful in defending her country against the Romans and Egypt became a possession of the Roman Empire.

With the coming of the Ptolemaic line after Alexander and the later conquest by the Romans, Egyptian culture, at least on the highest levels, underwent change. The ruling classes brought a whole range of new customs to every aspect of life in Egypt, from architecture to costume (Fig. 10). In the tomb of an official named Petosiris the traditional representations of the activities of the estate depict people dressed as Greeks but still illustrating the important tasks of cultivation and food preparation. Preserved in the Greco-Roman Museum at Alexandria is a painting of a traditional scene of animals driving a sakieh (waterwheel), but the painting style is Greco-Roman, not Egyptian (Fig. 11). Perhaps one of the most telling illustrations of the combination of divergent traditions is the painted mummy portrait. Customarily the face of the deceased had been covered with

FIGURE 10   Sarcophagi and other monuments in classical style. Ptolemaic to Roman Periods
The Greco-Roman Museum in Alexandria. These objects symbolize the domination of Egypt by foreign powers late in its history and the introduction of artistic
concepts that were un-Egyptian.
Author's photograph

FIGURE 11   Greco-Roman fresco. Ptolemaic to Roman Periods
From a tomb near Alexandria, this painting depicts cattle driving a waterwheel
(sakieh), a device that came to Egypt late in its history.
Author's photograph

a modeled, three-dimensional mask. In the time of the Romans in Egypt this was often replaced with a realistic painting on a flat wood panel. The mummy of a young man named Artimidoris, preserved in the British Museum, exemplifies this blending of customs in that the face is a naturalistic portrait and the body covering is decorated with traditional images of the ancient Egyptian gods.

In summary, the history of Egypt is reflected in the long development of the arts, crafts, and materials used in the life of the people. An appreciation of this complex evolution must be based on both the artistic and physical evidence, always keeping in mind that we are at the mercy of accidents of preservation. Often assumptions must be made on incomplete information and care must be taken not to move too quickly to conclusions.

Bagnall, Roger S. *Egypt in Late Antiquity*. Princeton, NJ: Princeton University Press, 1993.

Bowman, Alan K. *Egypt After the Pharaohs 332 BC–AD 642: From Alexander to the Arab Conquest*. Berkeley: University of California Press, 1986.

Grimal, Nicolas. *A History of Ancient Egypt*. Oxford: Blackwell, 1992.

Herodotus. *Histories*. Translated by A. D. Godley. Cambridge, MA: Harvard University Press, 1963–1969.

Kemp, Barry J. *Ancient Egypt: Anatomy of a Civilization*. London: Routledge, 1989.

Redford, Donald B., ed. *The Oxford Encyclopedia of Ancient Egypt*. Oxford: Oxford University Press, 2001.

Shaw, Ian, ed. *The Oxford History of Ancient Egypt*. Oxford: Oxford University Press, 2000.

Silverman, David P., ed. *Ancient Egypt*. New York: Oxford University Press, 1997.

3

Study of the Material World of Ancient Egypt

This glimpse into the old world teaches us much.... The progress of civilization, the inventions of mankind have changed but little.

ADOLF ERMAN

The study of ancient Egypt and ancient Egyptian culture has most often concentrated on the language, history, religion, and prominent monuments. Certainly attention has been paid to the activities of the Egyptians and the objects and processes that made them possible, but not to the same degree. With some rare exceptions archaeologists and historians did not always treat the ordinary tools and utensils with the consideration they deserved. To properly understand the material world in which the Egyptians lived and worked, the emphasis has to be redirected to a certain extent to remedy this. Still, there are bits and pieces of information embedded in histories and narratives that bear reexamination.

It is only natural that those things that made the ancient Egyptians seem different or unusual should command the most attention – pyramids and mummies being the most familiar examples. From the Greek and Roman authors and travelers to the present day, the emphasis, when examining and discussing Egypt, has been to a great extent on the spectacular, the unusual, and the mysterious. Herodotus, writing in the fifth century BCE, went to lengths to describe the country, its geography, and its history as he understood it. He also concerned himself with Egyptian religion and the gods and how they related to the customs and beliefs of the Greeks, but when he came to a discussion of activities and customs, he stressed differences, in part to emphasize some similarities.

To understand the descriptions of the land of Egypt and Egyptian customs found in Herodotus' *Histories* it is important to remember that everything cannot be taken literally and that his emphasis of differences was for a kind of literary effect. He tells us that the Egyptians shun the use of Greek customs, as well as the customs of any other peoples, and that their customs and laws are for the most part different from those of all other men. He gives some detailed examples.

According to Herodotus Egyptian women buy and sell in the market and men stay home and weave. Men carry loads on their head, women on their shoulders. Egyptian priests shave their heads while elsewhere priests have their hair long. A number of other examples continue to emphasize the unique character of the Egyptians. Taking into consideration his desire to underline the differences and the fact that he wrote in the time of the Persian occupation near the end of Egypt's greatness, some of his observations are probably correct, but many call for skepticism and a critical examination.

One instance in which Herodotus does give an insightful description is in that of the craft of boatbuilding. He described that the planks were laid like courses of bricks, with the joints alternating, and that the boats had no ribs. In examination of preserved boats, these details seem to be correct (II, 96).

However useful Herodotus and most of the other ancient authors are in regard to descriptions of the monuments and other aspects of the country in their time, they have left little useful and reliable information about everyday activities and materials. It is not until almost the beginning of the nineteenth century that a serious interest in the minutia of everyday activity began to take hold. In the intervening centuries there were a number of European travelers who voyaged to Egypt, marveled at the ancient monuments, and often wrote memoirs of their experience. After 1516, when Egypt was conquered by the Ottoman Turks, it became certainly easier and safer for foreigners to visit the country, so the period from the sixteenth to the eighteenth centuries saw a number of distinguished persons who made the trip.

The widespread interest of early travelers and their countries of origin can be illustrated by a small sampling that includes the Swiss Felix Fabri in 1483, the Frenchman Pierre Belon in 1547, and the Englishman George Sandys in 1611. In the beginning of the seventeenth century the study of the pyramids was advanced by Pietro delle Valle, an Italian nobleman, who described them as they were in 1615, but it was up to an English astronomer and mathematician named John Greaves to do the most accurate survey of those monuments that had been accomplished to his time. Greaves traveled to Egypt in 1639 and published his study of the pyramids in 1646, a work surpassing in observation and accuracy anything on the subject previously attempted. In 1738–39 the separate expeditions of two travelers, Frederick Norden, a Danish naval officer, and Richard Pococke, an English clergyman, crossed paths on the Nile. They both left lively accounts of their travels that, when taken together, provide an extensive series of descriptions of the monuments, customs, and life of the people they encountered. Norden left one of the earliest accurate images of the Great Sphinx; Pococke made the first attempt at a map of the Valley of the Kings at Thebes.

As interesting as many of the descriptions and accounts left by these travelers and others who visited Egypt may be, there was very little possibility for such visitors to know or understand the rudiments of the life of the ancient Egyptians. The illustrations of the monuments included in their publications range from accurate renderings to almost imaginary concoctions. Even so, they can still serve in many cases to depict the condition of the remains and the sites as they were in their own day.

In 1798 Napoleon Bonaparte invaded Egypt with a French expeditionary force numbering about 45,000 under his command. What made the French expedition so important to the further study of ancient Egypt was that Napoleon added a large group of scholars, artists, and engineers to his military force. They were given the tasks of studying and mapping the country; they recorded not only the flora and fauna and aspects of agricultural and domestic activity of their time, but they paid great attention to the ancient monuments as well.

The Description of Egypt, the mammoth multivolume publication eventually produced by this expeditionary group, was the most thorough study of a non-European country attempted to that time. It was divided into three sections, Antiquity, Natural History, and The Modern State. The Egyptian campaign left such a lasting influence on the study of the ancient civilization that it has been called "the birth of Egyptology." The drawings and engravings of the monuments made by the French are often the only accurate renderings of structures that have since been damaged and in some cases even totally destroyed, but the illustrations in the section on antiquity were mainly concerned with what were considered major monuments. There were, in addition, plates that illustrated statues and small objects such as amulets, scarabs, and texts on papyrus, but the great majority of the illustrations were architectural renderings of temples and tombs.

An important source of information about ancient Egypt comes from the representations in the tombs of the elite classes, where many of the activities of the estate and the field are illustrated. In the *Description* only a limited number of such tombs were sampled and the record of such scenes is consequently small. Some vignettes of farming activities, such as plowing, sowing, and reaping, are included, with a small number of examples of tools and clothing. Processing and storage of the grain is also shown. Examples of musicians and their instruments, papyrus boatbuilding, and some other areas of food preparation are also recorded, but almost all of these are shown as if they were isolated designs and not parts of elaborately decorated tomb walls. The French expedition's emphasis on what they considered major monuments can be demonstrated by the fact that many of the examples of tomb painting used in the publication came from the tombs at El Kab in the south and Beni Hasan in Middle Egypt, both in areas where there were few significant examples of standing stone architecture and the French artists had the time to turn their attention to the study of the tomb paintings. It was not until the early nineteenth century that the paintings and reliefs in many tombs would be found, examined, and recorded in detail.

The immediate aftermath of the Napoleonic campaign ushered in a period of systematic collecting of antiquities on a large scale. The developing museums of Europe in London, Paris, Rome, and Turin, in northern Italy, all benefited from the ease with which their representatives were able to procure ancient objects to furnish their collections. The government of Mohammad Ali (1769–1849) allowed representatives of foreign nations to excavate and collect almost without restriction.

Notable among the agents employed by Henry Salt, the English consul, was an Italian expatriate named Giovanni Belzoni who worked in Egypt from 1815 to 1819 (Fig. 12). He was an able engineer who became a specialist in the transportation of monumental sculpture. He was also, in some respects, a pioneer archaeologist. From Belzoni's memoirs it seems clear that he understood the rudiments of stratigraphy and its use in establishing the sequence of remains and artifacts in an excavation. He also understood that the artifacts he discovered could begin to reveal much about the life of the ancients.

The Egyptians were certainly well acquainted with linen manufacture to a perfection equal to our own; for in many of their figures, we observe their garments quite transparent; and among the folding of the mummies, I observed some cloth quite as fine as our common muslin, quite strong, and of an even texture. They had the art of tanning leather, with which they made shoes as well as we do, some of which

FIGURE 12   Giovanni Belzoni, an early excavator and treasure hunter.
Belzoni saw that the objects he found could provide information about life in antiquity. Much reviled as a vandal who opened tombs with a battering ram, Belzoni excavated, preserved, and recorded what he found.

> I found of various shapes. They also had the art of staining the leather with various colours, as we do Morocco, and actually knew the mode of embossing on it, for I found leather with figures impressed on it, quite elevated. I think it must have been done with a hot iron while the leather was wet. (Belzoni, pp. 269–270)

Belzoni further observed the following:

> In all my researches I found only one arrow, two feet long. At one extremity it had a copper point well fixed in, and at the other a notch as usual to receive the string of the bow: it had been evidently split by the string, and glued together again. (Belzoni, p. 268)

Although Belzoni was principally interested in acquiring important sculpture for his employer (and for himself) he exhibited a remarkable

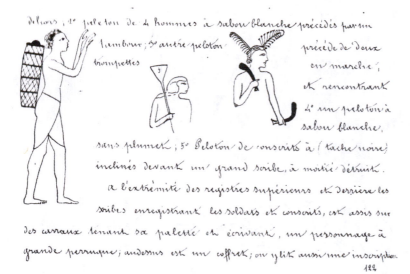

FIGURE 13   **Page detail from J. F. Champollion's** *Monuments de'Égypte et de la Nubie: notices descriptive* **(1835–47).**
This detail illustrates a military drummer and trumpeter, copied from a tomb painting. Champollion, on his expedition to Egypt, not only copied inscriptions but noted interesting details such as these.

degree of insight in interpreting the useful objects of antiquity that he happened on. He is often characterized as a looter who opened tombs with a battering ram, and some of his methods would not always be approved today. However, his understanding of what he found far exceeded that of most of his contemporaries.

In 1828–29 Ippolito Rosellini and Jean François Champollion, the decipherer of hieroglyphs, led a joint French-Tuscan mission to Egypt. The members of the group had the advantage of being the first researchers who could certainly read the ancient language, recognize the names of kings, and establish some sense of a historical chronology. Unlike the scholars and artists who were a part of the Napoleonic campaign that preceded them, this group had a more focused purpose, which was to concentrate on the antiquities and to make more accurate plans and renderings of what they saw. Also unlike their predecessors, and because they were not part of an invading army, they could travel at their own pace and had more time to devote to their aim of accuracy and to the examination of the decoration of private tombs, which illustrated various activities (Figs. 13, 14).

Rosellini and Champollion worked separately, each with his own crew of artists and draftsmen, but they conferred and collaborated, so the results show evidence of a joint effort. The publications of

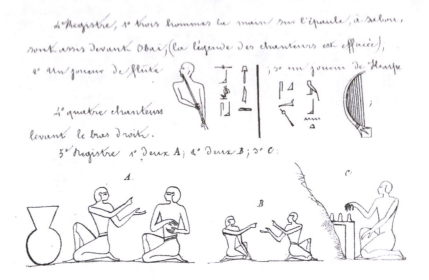

FIGURE 14   Page detail from J. F. Champollion's *Monuments de 'Égypte et de la Nubie: notices descriptive* (1835–47).
This illustration includes musicians, instruments, and singers.

the two scholars set an early standard for accuracy and complete-ness and became an inspiration for those who came after them. In the process they provided much more visual information about how the ancient Egyptians depicted agriculture, aspects of manufacture, and many other parts of life, from warfare to games. How they dif-fered was in a basic approach to the recording of tomb decoration. Where Champollion recorded the reliefs and paintings as complete tableaus, illustrating the layout and arrangements of tomb walls, Rosellini gathered illustrations of specific aspects of ancient culture he had extracted from the representations on the walls of many dif-ferent tombs. As an example, he took the subject "birds of ancient Egypt" and grouped all the different species that he and his artists had observed in many locations. In the same way he put together many different images depicting a craft, such as woodworking or weaving, regardless of the specific place of origin or the period in which the images were created, better explaining how each activity was carried out because of the varied sources and depictions. As a result, Rosellini can be considered one of the first scholar-explorers to be especially concerned with recording and explaining the material world of the ancients and not just the monumental remains of Egypt. He was also the first to use color in his publication of tomb paintings.

Both Rosellini and Champollion and their artists and draftsmen produced hundreds of drawings and collected hundreds of objects to the benefit of mainly the Archaeological Museum in Florence and the Louvre Museum in Paris. The two multivolume publications that were eventually produced recorded their extensive travels in Egypt and Nubia and provided new and accurate information for the generations of scholars who followed them.

Inspired by the work of his two predecessors and their publications, which were just beginning to appear, Karl Richard Lepsius led a Prussian expedition to Egypt in 1842–45 to continue the study and recording of the monuments. He was better funded, better equipped, and had a larger staff than the two earlier scholars. The drawings and plans produced by the group were clearly more accurate as a result. The plates in the twelve volumes of his *Monuments of Egypt and Ethiopia* still provide scholars a reliable reference to the temples and tombs and their decoration that exceeds the work of those that had gone before, especially in the area of tomb paintings that depict everyday activity.

Lepsius and his group managed to collect about 15,000 objects and plaster casts, a scholarly treasure trove that provided the nucleus of the Berlin Museum collection, where he later became the keeper of the Egyptian section. This was not an accumulation of works of art only but included a wide variety of artifacts (pottery, furniture, tools, and weapons) that illustrate ordinary activities. Lepsius is considered the founder of German Egyptology, as are Rosellini for Italy and Champollion for France. Each of them contributed greatly to the study and understanding of life in ancient Egypt that goes beyond royal monuments and temples, and each provided, in their time, new and revealing information about the land, the people, and their activities.

Considering all the accomplishments of his three distinguished contemporaries, Sir John Gardner Wilkinson stands out as an explorer working alone. An Englishman who had once considered the navy and the clergy as career choices, he was influenced by the antiquarian Sir William Gell to study ancient Egypt and eventually he decided to investigate the country and monuments for himself. He lived and traveled in Egypt for twelve years (1821–33) with other later visits. Wilkinson, unlike the leaders of the three great expeditions, was not funded by any government or scientific society. He had contacts with the main developments in scholarship of the time through Gell, but he was self-driven to study the antiquities in all of their aspects.

Wilkinson spent most of his time in Thebes among the tombs on the west bank, and it was from his familiarity with the tomb

No. 254.   Sacred musicians, and a priest offering incense.   *Leyden Museum.*

FIGURE 15   **A page from Sir John Gardner Wilkinson's** *Manners and Customs of the Ancient Egyptians* **(1837).**
Wilkinson used tomb paintings to explain his subject. His drawings have proved to be generally accurate and continue to provide information about activities and customs.

decoration and the actual objects then being excavated that he derived knowledge of aspects of the ancients that had not been considered by other explorers in the same depth. The eventual result was a revolutionary publication that introduced a new way to study ancient life. Wilkinson's *The Manners and Customs of the Ancient Egyptians* (1837) (Fig. 15) was the first concerted attempt to go beyond temples and tombs, kings and mummies. The subtitle of the work tells it all: *Including Their Private Life, Government, Laws, Arts, Manufactures, Religion, Agriculture, and Early History, derived from a comparison of the painting, sculptures, and monuments still existing, with the accounts of the ancient authors.* Wilkinson's work was very popular in its time and went through a number of later editions. His discussion of a banquet illustrates how he attempted to make the Egyptians come alive to the reader:

> A circumstance of this kind is represented in a tomb at Thebes. A party, assembled at the house of a friend, are regaled with the sound of music, and the customary introduction of refreshments; and no attention which the host could show his visitors appears to be neglected on the occasion. The wine has circulated freely ... (Wilkinson, 1878 ed., vol. 2, p. 20)

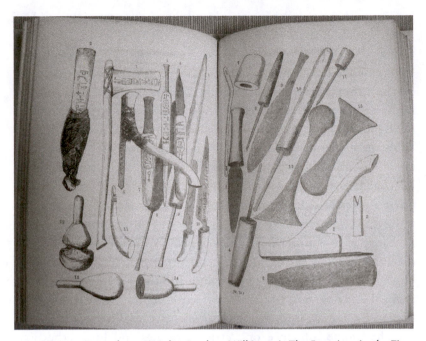

FIGURE 16   Pages from Sir John Gardner Wilkinson's *The Egyptians in the Time of the Pharaohs* (1857).
These are ancient objects that Wilkinson saw, examined, or collected. He was one of the early enthusiasts of ancient Egyptian life who studied ordinary objects and artifacts in detail.
Author's photograph

This was no longer a concentration on only dynasties, successions of rulers, battles, and conquests, but a vivid reconstruction of what life and customs among the Egyptians may have been. It was to set a pattern for many later works with similar emphasis (Fig. 16).

As the European interest in ancient Egypt grew, other scholars took Wilkinson's lead in the discussion of aspects of life in ancient Egypt. Notable among them was Adolf Erman, a distinguished German scholar, professor, and museum professional. His *Life in Ancient Egypt* was published in 1885 and translated into English in 1895. It is still in print and has served generations as an introduction to the general culture of ancient Egypt, as well as vividly illustrating aspects of daily life. As scholarly research and publication provided new information, and as modern means of communication developed, many more authors followed the lead of Wilkinson and Erman. A casual search on the Internet will currently yield around fifteen or twenty works with the title *Daily Life in Ancient Egypt* or something very similar.

The archaeological basis for the study of the material world of Egypt was also becoming more focused in the latter half of the nineteenth century. Alexander Rhind, a Scot, excavated in Thebes in the 1850s, well ahead of others of the period. He recognized that context and associations of finds and stratigraphy in an excavation were meaningful and important. His interesting collection of artifacts is in the Royal Scottish Museum, Edinburgh. But it was an Englishman, William Matthew Flinders Petrie, who revolutionized the developing discipline of Egyptology. Trained as a surveyor, Petrie as a young man had been a keen student of British archaeology. To prove or disprove a prophetic theory about the Great Pyramid at Giza, he went to Egypt in 1880 to do an accurate survey of the monument.

Petrie almost immediately developed an interest in the monuments and history of the country, and although mainly self-taught, he stayed on to excavate in Egypt and Palestine for more than sixty years. The last quarter of the nineteenth century was a period of intense development in the physical sciences, which certainly must have had some influence on Petrie's attitudes and his methods of work. He is usually credited with being the single innovator in the history of archaeology who saw the importance of detailed recording and careful preservation of the "ordinary" objects from excavations. Certainly he was convinced that the true study of antiquity was not only about statues and inscriptions, and that attention to the objects and materials ordinarily discarded by other excavators might yield a more complete picture of ancient culture and society. He was to pass this concern on to generations of Egyptologists and excavators, beginning with his many students and assistants.

Petrie's interests were almost encyclopedic. Metrology, the study of weights and measures, had an early and long-lasting fascination for him; the similarity of symbols and decorative devices in different cultures was another. In addition to his regular publication of his excavations (a practice not yet carried on by many of his contemporaries), he published by type many of the objects he had excavated or collected. The monographs written by Petrie included specialized works on objects of daily use, tools and weapons, slate palettes, Predynastic pottery, scarabs and seals, and funerary furniture, among other topics. He analyzed the material, charted stylistic differences, called attention to unusual features, and treated objects with the scholarly care that would produce a deeper understanding of the Egyptians.

Petrie made a practice of dividing objects from his excavations with supporting museums around the world. This insured that the ordinary objects he valued as significant evidence of Egyptian history would be exposed to a much wider public. A large part of his collections were left to what is now the Petrie Museum, University College, London, where they form one of the most extensive resources on ancient Egypt and especially on the ways that people lived and worked. His influence on the practice of excavation was profound. Not only did he teach others to observe and record, but he trained Egyptian workmen whose descendants are still carrying on the select occupation of archaeological excavation to this day. After Petrie the process of uncovering ancient remains was changed forever, and the knowledge of antiquity in its many aspects was expanded to include a greater sense of how people lived and acted.

From Napoleon's expedition at the end of the eighteenth century to Petrie's time, the explorers and scholars of ancient Egypt, its monuments, and its artifacts had become more attuned to the possibilities of knowing and understanding the material world of the ancient Egyptians. In 1982 the Museum of Fine Arts, Boston, organized an important exhibition titled *Egypt's Golden Age: The Art of Living in the New Kingdom, 1558–1085 BC*. This was an unusual attempt to document the lifestyles of Egypt in a particular period. Although it did not attempt a complete history of artifacts and objects from all of Egyptian history, it illustrated many of the object types used in everyday living.

Modern developments in the sciences have made many advances in archaeology possible. Today the situation is developing even further; excavation is not a one-man endeavor. Specialists in many different fields collaborate on the study of the material found, and the results can be far more rewarding to science and history. Something as simple as a segment of rope, when examined, can reveal that it was made of papyrus, flax, or grass, or even some other plant material, thus giving an insight into an industry and its adaptability to particular situations. Scientific analysis can determine if some materials are domestic or foreign, making it possible to chart areas of trade and production in the ancient world.

With satellite imaging and the Global Positioning System (GPS), distance sensing, ground radar, and ground receptivity, the discovery of and accurate mapping of sites have become far more accurate. Carbon 14 and thermoluminescent dating techniques (among others) have made it possible to assign more precise time periods to organic materials and to ceramic products, including pottery. The CT (computerized axial tomography) scan procedure has made it no longer crucial to use invasive and destructive techniques in the investigation of human remains. The electron microscope can produce detailed analysis of the elements contained in a specimen, making it possible to identify materials and their geographical origins more precisely. As a further example, the minute examination of grain, husks, and other plant residue has contributed to the study of ancient ecology and practices of cultivation, as well a better understanding of diet and nutrition.

With all of these scientific applications there is still a significant gradual advancement that has been made in the study of ancient Egypt that may seem obvious today but was slow to be recognized. The details of daily life, either evidenced by actual objects or represented in the visual arts, are important to any attempt to understand the culture of ancient Egypt. For too long the students of Egypt concentrated on unraveling the details of Egyptian history, the complexities of the language, the technical aspects of the architecture, and the stylistic development of the justly important works of art, to the exclusion of what it was that could shed light on the lives of the people. This is gradually being remedied. It is hoped that the following text will help to advance understanding of life and living in ancient Egypt.

It has become obvious in attempting to study the past through archaeology that no clue, no matter how small or seemingly insignificant, should be overlooked. A more complete understanding of an ancient civilization is comprised of more than just masterpieces preserved in museum galleries. Our knowledge of life in ancient Egypt and its remains has been conditioned and expanded by almost two hundred years of exploration. Our understanding of the artifacts, texts, and inscriptions has been subjected to constant clarification and revision by ongoing scholarly study, which continues today. As a result of all of these efforts, it is possible at the beginning of the twenty-first century to sketch a picture of the material world of ancient Egypt as never before.

Abt, Jeffrey. *American Egyptologist: The Life of James Henry Breasted and the Creation of His Oriental Institute.* Chicago: University of Chicago Press, 2011.

Breasted, Charles. *Pioneer to the Past; the Story of James Henry Breasted, Archaeologist.* New York: C. Scribner's Sons, 1943.

Fagan, Brian M. *The Rape of the Nile: Tomb Robbers, Tourists, and Archaeologists in Egypt.* New York: Scribner, 1975.

Greener, Leslie. *The Discovery of Egypt.* New York: Viking, 1967.

Peck, William H. "The Constant Lure" in *Ancient Egypt: Discovering Its Splendors*, edited by W. K. Simpson. Washington, DC: National Geographic Society, 1978. Pp. 9–24.

Wilson, John Albert. *Signs & Wonders Upon Pharaoh; a History of American Egyptology*. Chicago: University of Chicago Press, 1964.

Thousands of Years; an Archaeologist's Search for Ancient Egypt. New York: Scribner, 1972.

4

Dress and Personal Adornment

You are clothed in the robe of finest linen, the garments that clad the flesh of the god.

THE PRAYERS OF PAHERI

Do not covet copper, Disdain beautiful linen;
What good is one dressed in finery, If he cheats before the god?

THE INSTRUCTION OF AMENEMOPE

DRESS

Ideas of what constitutes dress or costume are as old and as varied as civilized humankind. The original impulse to don some sort of clothing can be explained in three ways: as the desire for protection of the body, to satisfy a developing sense of modesty, or as a need to display various kinds of social distinctions. Aspects of protection that might have determined the type of garments chosen include the need to combat the effects of climate, of heat and cold. The need for protection also includes the safeguarding of sensitive parts of the body, particularly the genital area. By contrast to the considerations of protection, a sense of modesty is a learned habit that demands concealment of various body parts, depending on the requirements or the traditions of the particular culture. In addition to the elements of protection and modesty, special types of costume and dress can provide the visual clues that differentiate social class and rank. The special costumes that are appropriate to different social positions and levels of authority utilize distinctive patterns and kinds of clothing for the male and female, and still other variations suitable for the young and old. Costume among the ancient Egyptians fulfilled these various requirements of protection, modesty, and social distinction in a variety of ways that can be studied in the sources preserved for us.

Much of our information about dress and costume comes from the representations in sculpture and wall decoration, but any attempt to understand Egyptian dress from these "illustrations" must take into consideration the conventions observed in Egyptian art. Egyptian artists worked within a tradition that was in essence conservative, meaning that they tended to look to accepted forms from the past. They had an ingrained tendency to repeat earlier and respected standards of representation. The primary religious intention of the depictions in a tomb demanded that the participants be shown in formal attire and in a reserved pose, and it is not at all certain that they dressed that way normally when carrying out ordinary affairs. There was no attempt to show the differences of dress for different seasons, effects of climate, or even different times of day. There is, however, strict attention paid to the representation of differences in class and rank.

In the symbolic language of Egyptian art things were not represented as they were seen but as they were best described and as they were meant to be understood for eternity. It has even been suggested that the depictions of attire we take to be typical of a historical period might more properly be "read" and recognized as representing the individual in a particular way for religious reasons. Taking these explanations into consideration, the lasting images of the ancient Egyptians are not to be seen as snapshots filled with easily decipherable information but are something closer to posed studio portraits in elaborate formal dress attired for a specific purpose. One of the best modern comparisons that can be made is with typical formal wedding photographs, where the bride and groom are shown in a specially chosen gown and a tuxedo, "costumes" that they would seldom wear in ordinary activities.

From what can be deduced based on evidence described in the following paragraphs, the daily costume of the ancient Egyptians seems to have been simple in the extreme (Fig. 17). The principal fabric employed throughout history was linen, processed from the flax plant. It is thought that flax was not originally native to Egypt but imported at an early date from the area of Syria. However, garments of linen are known from as early as the Predynastic Period. Flax was an important commodity in Egyptian culture not only for its use in clothing material; flax was also used as thread, rope, and woven matting. Wool was also used in the production of garments, more often than popularly believed, but cotton was unknown until about the first century CE. Animal hide, leather, and fur were also employed for some kinds of clothing, but there is less evidence for these materials, probably because they were more susceptible to damage from insects or humidity and fewer examples have been preserved. The belief that Egyptian clothing was always colorless, white, or off-white has been often overstated. In the past it was often thought that almost all Egyptian clothing was the color of the

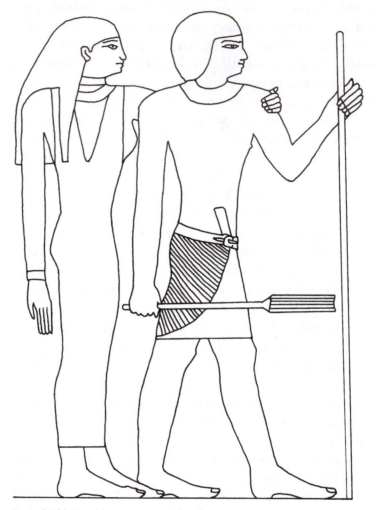

FIGURE 17   Typical Old Kingdom costume of the elite. Dynasties Five and Six
The male wears a short pleated kilt with a wig and beaded collar. The female wears
a close-fitting sheath dress and a wig and beaded collar as well.
Drawing by Duane Stapp

natural linen, demanding further embellishment with colored accessories, especially colored jewelry. From a range of preserved finds
it is clear that there were some colored fabrics or cloth with special
dyed parts, such as borders and fringes.

Spinning and weaving are well documented in tomb decoration and are also documented in great detail in models made for the
tomb. In the Middle Kingdom it had become a custom to represent
some of the activities previously shown on tomb walls by substitut-
ing elaborate models. These small tableaus of various crafts, made
of wood and painted plaster, are often remarkably detailed, so much
so that they furnish information that would otherwise be lost. In

the model of a weaver's shop from the tomb of a nobleman named Meketre, figures are presented carrying out the basic stages of making cloth: preparing the fibers, spinning thread, and finally weaving. This model includes an example of a horizontal loom, a possible answer to the question of whether Egyptian looms were horizontal or vertical.

Woven materials were produced in temple workshops, but there was also a household industry that was mainly carried out by women. Linen cloth was very important in Egyptian society and had multiple uses. In addition to clothing, linen was employed as a commodity that could be used in barter/trading and even to pay wages. A letter of a priest named Hekanakht illustrates the usefulness of cloth as an article of trade. He wrote:

> After it [a quantity of cloth] has been evaluated in the village of Nebeseyet, they should take it and rent farmland for what it is worth. (Wente, *Letters from Ancient Egypt*, p. 68, Dynasty Eleven)

The possession of quantities of linen cloth seems to have been an indication of rank, status, and wealth, to judge from the amounts found in some tombs. Stores of linen were often included in the tomb goods, and the amounts of cloth were listed in great quantities in the prayers for the spirit. Cloths, as a valued commodity, were routinely repaired and recycled. This is well illustrated in a letter from a man to his son:

> And you shall be attentive to take this rag of a kilt and this rag of a loin-cloth in order to rework the kilt into a red sash and the loincloth into an apron. (Wente, *Letters from Ancient Egypt*, p. 218, Dynasty Nineteen)

Clothing is mentioned in other letters as being recycled when it was beyond repair to be used as lamp wicks and as bandages for the living. An important evidence for this extended use of fabrics was the employment of worn and repaired material as mummy wrapping. Often the wrapping and padding material found on mummies shows signs of darning and patching, indicating that it had a long, useful life before being used as a part of the preparation of the dead. The mummy "bandages" are often clearly ripped from larger pieces and sometimes include the fringe or the selvage edges of the original. In some cases mummy wrappings have obvious signs of wear indicating reuse as well as what appear to be ownership marks or "laundry marks," further attesting to the practice of recycling.

The technology of weaving developed rapidly from Predynastic times to satisfy the demands of a growing population. However,

FIGURE 18   **A linen garment with a V-shaped neckline. Dynasty Eighteen**
Such garments, called tunics, were typically unisex – worn by both men and
women. The apparent shapelessness was remedied by the use of belts or sashes.
As part of an elaborate costume they functioned as an undergarment.
Photograph © The Trustees of the British Museum

most of the garments that were made of linen and have survived
are of amazingly simple design. The modern concepts of tailoring
to fit and standardized graduated sizes were virtually unknown to
the Egyptians. As a consequence most clothing was of a draped or
wraparound pattern, although a small number of shaped dresses and
other items with sleeves have been found (Fig. 18).

It is thought by some scholars that many of the excavated and
preserved examples of textiles have not been recognized as garments
and have been identified in the past as flat goods such as sheets, tow-
els, and shawls. As techniques of examination, identification, and
preservation have developed, a number of garments, garment parts,
and related materials have been "discovered" in museum storerooms,
adding to the body of evidence that makes up this study. From their
shape, size, and even preserved patterns of folding, kilts, loincloths,
wraparound dresses, and other costume pieces can sometimes be
recognized among previously misidentified specimens.

The principal types of garments worn by men and women were
the loincloth, kilt, skirt, dress, tunic, and a variety of head coverings

FIGURE 19   A scribe with his palette. Dynasty Eighteen
This fragment illustrates the elaborate costume and drapery of the
time of Tutankhamun. The layered and folded garment is a good
example of the complexity possible with relatively simple material.
The scribe has his palette tucked under his arm in a casual way; he
apparently was standing behind the chair of his master.
Courtesy of the Walters Art Museum

(Figs. 19, 20). These were "accessorized" with shawls, cloaks, sashes,
and aprons.

The loincloth was the unisex item of underwear for the
Egyptians, worn by males and females alike. It was a triangular
shape of linen, usually made of two smaller triangles joined on a
median line. It was worn tied around the waist with the long side
across the back and brought up between the legs, where the third
point was secured to the other two. Although the loincloth was
used principally as an undergarment for the upper classes, it is usually represented in painting and relief carving as the single item of

FIGURE 20   **New Kingdom costume of various classes. Dynasty Eighteen**
Theban Tomb 69, tomb of Menena
Senior scribes on the left wear tunics, kilts, and semitransparent overkilts. Junior
scribes on the right wear only tunics with kilts. Workmen in the center wear only
kilts.
Author's photograph

apparel for workmen in the fields, except in the cases where they wore nothing at all. The tomb of Tutankhamun contained a supply of about fifty loincloths, suggesting the importance of this item of apparel to everyday life.

A special variety of loincloth made of soft, thin leather was worn by some classes of workmen as an outside garment. These were made of skins or hides artfully pierced with small slits to create a network effect that almost suggests a fabric. From the depiction of these extraordinary items in tomb paintings they seem to have been favored by foreign ethnic types from lands south of Egypt (Fig. 21).

Additional information about the various kinds of garments used by the Egyptians is of an unusual type, furnished by a group of ostraca, fragments of pottery or flakes or chips of limestone, from the New Kingdom workers' village of Deir el Medina. These fragments, with their flat and regular surfaces, were ideal substitutes for papyrus, and they were often used for writing and drawing. On one such ostracon an ancient Egyptian has drawn sketches of various

FIGURE 21   A leather loincloth. New Kingdom
This garment was made by carefully slitting the animal skin in an
intricate pattern that resembles weaving. These garments are often
depicted in tomb paintings as worn by workmen, particularly those
who appear to be foreigners.
Photograph © The Trustees of the British Museum

pieces of clothing. Some of them can be identified as representing
loincloths, bag tunics, and sashes. Others are simple rectangles, with
and without fringes. The French excavator Bernard Bruyère suggested that the drawings may represent inventories of materials to
be put into a tomb. It is equally possible to imagine that they might
have been the equivalent of itemized laundry lists instead, complete
with illustrations.

In addition to the different kinds of clothing listed previously
there is a special garment described by some scholars as the "archaic
wraparound." This is best known from its representation on the
Narmer Palette, from the beginning of Egyptian history. It consists
of a wraparound piece of apparel that is tied over one shoulder and
covers the torso from the chest to the knees. This one-shouldered

garment was sometimes worn by men and women alike, but its limited popularity died out in Dynasty Four, and it appears only sporadically thereafter, usually in representations of ritual situations. The design did not widely persist in Egyptian fashion perhaps because the one-shoulder effect offended the Egyptian love of symmetry. There are, however, other examples of one-shouldered garments, especially one made of panther skin that functioned as an insignia of priesthood.

The kilt and skirt were standard items of dress with many variations. The male kilt in the Old Kingdom varied in length, but it was usually represented at about knee length for the average prosperous man and below the knee for individuals of higher rank or advanced age. This automatically suggests that the longer, more formal kilt was adopted to portray dignity, importance, and rank in the community. In some tombs the deceased was seen in different representations as attired in both styles of kilts, characterizing him at two distinct times in life: as young and athletic and as older and socially important and influential. In either case the kilt was a wraparound, like a sarong that was wound one or more times around the torso and secured by tucking the loose end in at the waist. This was sometimes made more secure by the addition of a sash held by a tied knot. The tucked end of the kilt is often represented in sculpture and, because it is occasionally designed as an actual rectangular tab, is sometimes misunderstood as the handle of a knife.

In the Old Kingdom women are usually represented in simple sheath-like dresses with or without shoulder straps. In sculpture and two-dimensional depictions of this garment it is so closely form-fitting as to call to mind a flexible body stocking. Occasionally a V-shaped neckline is indicated. In some two-dimensional depictions one breast is exposed, but this is an artistic convention meant to convey the idea that females have breasts. There are some problems with interpreting this garment, even though it was the standard way to represent female wear in this period. No known preserved complete examples of such a garment have been identified. As it is usually shown, such a sheath dress would have limited ordinary activities and almost hobbled the wearer by its design. It is argued by some scholars that what looks like a sheath dress is a representational simplification of a wraparound-type dress meant to emphasize the characteristics of the female figure. The illustration of sheath dresses is difficult to understand, especially since examples of this type of tight-fitting dress have not been found.

The male kilt and the female sheath dress are ideal means to represent and emphasize the characteristics of masculinity and femininity (Fig. 17). The manner in which they are depicted in art accomplishes this but does not offer easy explanations for the construction of the garments. In three-dimensional sculpture and two-dimensional painting and relief carving the sheath dress is the standard female garment throughout the Old Kingdom and into the Middle Kingdom. For men of rank or position in the Middle Kingdom formal wear often includes a more impressive longer kilt, extending from just below the chest to the ankles.

In the New Kingdom, Egyptian costume is represented as being much more elaborate than it had been before, at least for the privileged classes. Where previously garments had been relatively simple, here complexity became fashionable. Pleats and folds, multilayering, and complicated draping became the norm. Garments made of particularly fine linen are shown as transparent, revealing undergarments and the figures of the wearers. The elaborate costumes of the New Kingdom became so specialized that it is possible to assign precise periods and dates to some sculpture on the basis of changes in design.

Representations of children before they have reached the age of puberty usually show them as completely naked. After puberty they are depicted in costumes similar to adult wear. These conventions may be a symbolic way of illustrating the age difference and immaturity, and it is likely that small children wore some kind of clothes. Many types of adult field workers are also traditionally shown as nude. It is possible that total nudity was not the norm in real life, considering the demands of the climate in Egypt, and this convention probably had to do with age for the children and with status for the workmen rather than the demands of a particular occupation. An exception to this idea may be the nudity of female entertainers. Dancers and some musicians at banquets are often represented as nude or nearly nude.

It should be repeated and emphasized that the depictions of clothing on the walls of tombs and temples does not represent normal everyday activity but a kind of formal ideal. It is hard to imagine that male royalty and members of the nobility in the Old Kingdom went "shirtless" in the harsh climate of Egypt and that women of the same time wore dresses that virtually hobbled them. As previously observed, the manner in which they were presented was meant to identify and emphasize the distinctions between male and female, as well as display masculine strength and feminine beauty. In the same way it is hardly possible that the elaborate costumes of the New Kingdom were everyday wear. The multilayered and complex pleating of the fabrics suggests attire that was reserved for special uses, whether for ceremony in life or for eternity and the next life.

FACIAL HAIR AND TATTOOING

We normally imagine ancient Egyptian males to be completely clean-shaven, but this was not always the case. The most obvious example of facial hair is the "false beard," a standard symbol of royalty or kingship. The symbolism of this emblematic beard is related to concepts of virility and strength. It is clear from representations in sculpture, relief, and painting that the long, sometimes plaited, almost cylindrical beard shape on the faces of kings was an item of royal regalia. The strap for this attachment is often indicated or implied in painting and sculpture. Standard representations of deities display a false beard of slightly different form, in which the tip curls up. In the Old and New Kingdoms there are examples of noblemen or dignitaries who wear a short beard similar to a goatee, but actual facial hair never seemed to gain lasting popularity in ancient Egypt.

However, there are some exceptions to the rule. In Dynasty Four in the Old Kingdom (and occasionally at later times) a neatly trimmed moustache was briefly popular for royalty as well as for members of the elite classes. Typical examples are the painted statue of a man named Rahotep, in the Cairo Museum, which has a striking moustache, as well as various images of King Menkaure in Cairo and the Museum of Fine Arts, Boston, where traces of color indicate that moustaches were intended. From the Middle Kingdom a number of mummy masks have been preserved that show the deceased with both moustache and neatly shaped beard. A significant exception to the completely hairless male face was the display of a growth of unshaved stubble in times of mourning the dead, occasionally even on royal images. This custom of not shaving in times of mourning is still observed in some cultures and religions, such as in some sects of Orthodox Judaism.

There is evidence of tattooing found on some mummies and in some representations in the decorative arts. In one case a female musician displays a tattooed image of the dwarf god Bes drawn on her thigh. On mummies much simpler examples of tattooing have been found, such as dots and circles marking the arms, thighs, abdomen, or chin. These body markings may relate to specific classes of individuals, such as dancers and entertainers, or they may be related to the observation of specific cults, such as those of Hathor or the dwarf god Bes.

COSMETICS

There is more detailed evidence for the use of cosmetics in Egypt than anywhere else in the ancient world. The use of cosmetics is well attested from the earliest times in the Predynastic Period, and cosmetics were particularly important to the Egyptians for practical purposes as well as for beautification. Since bathing was probably practiced in Egypt more commonly than in some other cultures, and the hot climate was harsh, there was more necessity for the use of oils and ointments to counter the effects of heat, dust, and the consequent dryness.

Egyptians of both sexes lined their eyes, painted their lips, and rouged their cheeks. Although it cannot be proved that cosmetics were invented in Egypt, the Egyptians were among the early cultures devoted to facial enhancement. The evidence for this includes the artistic representations on tomb walls, remains of actual materials, and the large numbers of preserved containers and related apparatus for the application of cosmetics. The special containers alone, consisting of jars, pots, tubes, and boxes, attest to the widespread use of makeup. Not only have the individual containers been found but so have examples of fitted boxes ("cosmetics kits") meant to hold the mirrors, jars, razors, and applicators.

The main difference between the ancient preparations and most cosmetics today is in the basic materials used. Modern cosmetics usually contain what are termed essential oils (various plant oils with a distinctive fragrance), generally mixed or suspended in an alcohol base, while the ancient preparations were made of oils and fats impregnated with the essence of plants, herbs, and spices.

Color to line the eyes was used by men and women alike, and it is thought that the Egyptians discovered that lining the eyelids gave some relief from the harsh sun to which they were exposed on a daily basis. The supposed medicinal benefits of eye cosmetics also go beyond simple protection from the sun. This is illustrated in the following excerpt from a letter of a draftsman to his son:

> May you bring me a bit of honey for my eyes as well as ochre that has been freshly molded (into sticks) and genuine galena.... I am searching

for my eyesight, but it no longer exists. (Wente, *Letters from Ancient Egypt*, p. 185, Dynasty Nineteen)

However it was used, eyeliner was clearly a standard type of makeup for aesthetic reasons. A long cosmetic line is often shown in paintings and on stone sculpture extending well beyond the corners of the eye. The minerals used for eyeliner included galena, a gray or black lead sulfide; malachite, a green copper carbonate; as well as carbon black, and more rarely, stibnite, a gray antimony sulfide. The types of small stone palettes known from the earliest times were used as a surface on which to grind the material to a powder so that it could be mixed into a paste for application. The great number of these palettes that exist from the Predynastic Period attest to the fact that the custom of painting or lining the eyes was widespread and as old as Egyptian civilization. Such palettes became decorative objects and were often made in the shapes of animals, birds, and reptiles.

Henna is a red dye made from the powdered leaves of a tropical shrub or flowering tree. In antiquity it was used to color the hair and occasionally to dye the hands and feet. Red hair on mummies such as that of the Pharaoh Ramesses II has been found after analysis to be artificially colored with henna. The significance of coloring the hands and feet, as has been found on other mummies, is not completely understood, but it may have something to do with making the body appear more lifelike, or it may have simply been considered an attractive decoration for the living. Other materials used in the care of the hair were oils, unguents, and grease, probably in order to counteract effects of the dry climate of Egypt.

In the so-called "Turin Erotic Papyrus," preserved in the Egyptian Museum in Turin, Italy, there is a clear representation of a woman holding a mirror and a brush in the act of painting her lips. Red powders have also been found that suggest that they were the materials used to color the cheeks. Cosmetic preparations have been discovered in powdered form, as cakes, as dried residue in the bottoms of containers made of a variety of materials, including seashells, as well as on mummified bodies. However, two aspects of cosmetic-related preparations can be attested to only by the texts in medical papyri (a discussion of these documents can be found in the chapter on medicine and hygiene). These two "cures" deal with remedying baldness and treating wrinkles. It is rather telling to discover that the ancient Egyptians had some of the same vanity-related concerns about aging that still exist today. In the *Ebers Papyrus* there is a formula for an application made of various animal fats that purports to cure baldness; in the *Edwin Smith Papyrus* there is a treatment titled "Making an Old Man Young Again" that was meant to solve the problem of the wrinkled skin of old age.

From the large amount of evidence preserved it is obvious that cosmetics, makeup, and attention to general skin care were of great importance to the ancient Egyptians. The procurement of mineral and plant materials; the preparation, refinement, and combination of them; and the trade and commerce that resulted could amount to a minor industry. However, it is difficult to identify occupations devoted exclusively to cosmetics and toiletries. From as early as the Middle Kingdom there are tomb representations of perfume makers who process flowers, but the existence of professional "cosmeticians," as they might be termed today, is doubtful. As yet, no depictions of one person applying eyeliner or other preparations to the face of another are known. The only examples that suggest specialized "beauticians" illustrate hairdressers at work.

CLOTHING CARE

> The washerman's day is going up, going down. All his limbs are weak, [from] whitening his neighbors' cloths every day, from washing their linen. (Papyrus Lansing, Lichtheim, *Ancient Egyptian Literature*, Vol. 2, p. 169)

The care of clothing included washing, repair, and storage. There are numerous tomb scenes of cloth being washed on the bank of a canal or the Nile River. The washer man used a stick or club to pummel the material while wet and squeezed the excess water out by wringing, often aided by inserting a stick in the folds to act as a handle and facilitate the twisting process. Natron, the natural soda found in the wadis in the desert, was used as a detergent and is mentioned in documents asking for supplies for the washer men. When the washing process was finished the clothing was spread on the river bank, grass, or bushes to dry and bleach in the sun. When the linen was properly cleaned it was off-white in color, of a hue that can best be described as light oatmeal. The brown color of mummy linen is the result of it not being exposed to the sun for centuries. Examples of linen wrapping that have been left out of doors from plundered tombs or graves gradually return to the lighter color from natural bleaching.

It is still not clearly understood how the process of the elaborate pleating of ancient garments was carried out. The preparation of the complex draped costumes of the New Kingdom would have been extremely labor intensive without some kind of practical aid or device. Boards have been found that are cut with a series of parallel ridges that are thought to have been used to position the pleats, but this is not at all certain. Doubtless pleating was done when the material was still damp, and the pleats, especially in linen garments, would set when dry. There has been discussion that a starch of some kind may have been used to make the pleats last, but this has not been satisfactorily proved either.

WIGS AND OTHER HEAD COVERINGS

In the climate of Egypt, with high degrees of heat in summer and constant exposure to the sun, it was obviously required to have some kind of protection for the head. The idea of a shaped hat did not seem to have appealed to the ancient Egyptians, even though it is well attested in some other ancient cultures. Hats as we know them did not exist in Egypt, but two other solutions were easily found. The first consisted of draped and tied cloth head coverings and the second of elaborate wigs. The head cloths took a variety of shapes and styles, from the formal *nemes* headdress of the king to the baglike covering seen on the heads of women who winnowed grain. The former was an attribute of kingship and the latter probably a practical way to keep grain dust out of the hair. The use of wigs requires a more complicated explanation

There are many different types of individual hair or wig styles represented in Egyptian art, and most of these can be seen to be restricted to particular social classes (Fig. 22). Modes of arranging or dressing the hair varied according to sex, age, rank, or station, and this is reflected not only in tomb representations but also in actual examples of wigs that have been preserved. The custom of wearing a wig that could be dressed in advance and donned when it was appropriate possibly explains the many complex hairstyles so often illustrated in the New Kingdom.

It is commonly assumed from available evidence that the wigs worn by the ancient Egyptians were the most popular form of head cover, but it is also true that there are many depictions of men and women in sculpture and tomb painting who are not wearing wigs. For the most part they represent people of the working classes, as contrasted to those of the elite, who were presented in

FIGURE 22   New Kingdom costume. Dynasty Eighteen
              Theban Tomb 55, tomb of Ramose
              The elaborate wigs of the elite class clearly show a two-tiered or
              double wig for the male and long heavy wig kept in place by a circlet
              for the female.
              Author's photograph

more formal attire wearing wigs. With this discussion of hairstyles
and wigs, however, it is well to remember that people of rank are
always shown in an ideal or formal situation, whereas depictions
of the less important people can be rendered in a more naturalistic
manner.

In some cases it is clear that what seems to be the natural hair can
be seen peeking from under the edge of a wig that does not completely cover it, as in the brightly colored statue of the lady Nofret, in
the Cairo Museum. It seems to have been a matter of personal choice
whether a person shaved the head or not. It has been suggested that
this was a matter of ritual cleanliness rather than style for priests,
and many priests are depicted with clean-shaven heads. It has been
seen that shaved heads for the clergy or the priesthood were a mark
of distinction in some ancient cultures other than ancient Egypt, a
characteristic that tends to mark the religious officiants as different
and set apart from the ordinary laypeople.

Wigs, and perhaps false beards, were constructed mainly of
human hair over a netting base made of either linen or other hair,

FIGURE 23   **A double wig arrangement of human hair. Dynasty Eighteen**
This preserved example illustrates the elaborate treatment of two styles of hair
dressing combined that was popular in the New Kingdom.
Photograph © The Trustees of the British Museum

and arranged and set with resin or beeswax (Fig. 23). It is sometimes
assumed (and occasionally stated in the literature) that animal hair
may have been used in the production of wigs; from actual investigation of the few examples that have been analyzed, this has not
been found to be the case. Some plant fiber has been found to have
been used as filler, but no horse or other animal hair has been discovered, contrary to this popular misconception. A limited number
of actual examples of wigs have been found from as early as Dynasty
Eleven in the Middle Kingdom, while some others from Dynasty
Twelve have been discovered in their original storage boxes. Since
wigs probably were considered items of formal wear, this shows that
they were carefully protected when not in use. There are a number
of wigs preserved in museum collections, but the frequent representations in art give much more information as to style and general appearance. In general use women's wigs were usually simpler

than those of men, giving rise to the suggestion that woman's hair-styles seem more natural and less artificial, but there were elaborate types of wigs for women as well, although these seem to have been designed for festival celebrations.

In the Old Kingdom men are occasionally shown with close-cropped natural hair, as can be seen in the statues of Rahotep, previously mentioned, and on a statue of Hemiunu, the architect of the Great Pyramid. However, the variety of possible styles in the same period is well illustrated on the group of wood panels from the tomb of Hesire, where he is depicted with a tightly curled wig, a full, flowing wig, and other styles. The visual effects of wearing a wig are graphically illustrated in two statues that were made for the same man. In two images Ranofer is shown with and without a wig, and although the two faces are nearly identical, the impression given by the two styles of hair dressing make his two statues look like two different individuals.

Men's wigs in the Old Kingdom tend to be of simple design, whatever the style. By contrast, in the New Kingdom they become more elaborate, often with one type of curls set over another. Women's wigs tend to be rather more straightforward, with rows of layered curls as well as braids and ringlets. They vary in length and often are long enough to cover the shoulders. Often the female wig is held in place by a circlet, usually a decorated band of flowers or even of precious metal. For the New Kingdom there is hardly a better series of examples of flower circlets than the relief carvings in the tomb of Ramose, of Dynasty Eighteen. By contrast to flowing wigs held in place by a circlet, in the time of Akhenaten and Nefertiti, at the end of Dynasty Eighteen, there is a particular style of close-fitting, short wig that has been termed "Nubian," favored by the queen and other female members of the court. It seems to have been an import from the south, hence the name.

Actual methods of hairdressing are occasionally illustrated in Egyptian art. On the sarcophagus of Lady Kawit, of Dynasty Eleven, found at Deir el Bahri, she is shown having her hair done by a servant or attendant. Cosmetic objects for the hair, including combs, pins, and curlers, have a long history and have been found in large quantities. Some of the earliest carved objects of ivory from the Predynastic Period are combs decorated with animal and bird shapes. Small scissor-shaped hair curlers of copper or bronze appear later, and hairpins exist from all periods.

FOOTWEAR

Send an oxhide or a goat skin! You shall give it, but only to the sandal maker Werniptah. And record it in writing that an oxhide has been given to the sandal maker. (Wente, *Letters from Ancient Egypt*, 86, Dynasty Twelve)

Their dress is entirely of linen,

and their shoes of the papyrus plant.

It is not lawful for them to wear either dress or shoes of any other material. (Herodotus, commenting about the costume of priests. *Histories*, Book II, p. 37)

From most of the artistic representations of people it is possible to get an impression that many ancient Egyptians went barefoot most of the time. While this is probably not the case, certainly footwear was not worn by much of the population. In a representation on the palette of King Narmer, from the beginning of Egyptian history, an attendant identified as his "sandal bearer" carries Narmer's footwear, implying that they were worn only for certain situations and removed in others.

Sandals were made of leather or of plant material such as papyrus and grasses. Leather sandals are known from as early as the Predynastic Period, and were often made of animal hide cut in such a way that base and straps were all made from the same piece. The hides of cattle, goats, and gazelle were used, and leather sandals might even be further decorated by dyeing the natural material. Preserved examples exhibit a variety of decorative treatments, including cut openwork designs and the use of different animal hides for contrasting textures.

The method of making sandals of papyrus or other fiber usually employed weaving, plaiting, or a technique called coiling, also used in basketry. In style they were very much like modern flip-flops, with a strap across the instep secured with a cord between the large and second toes. In the Ramesside Period, Dynasties Nineteen and Twenty, the elongated point of the toe could be turned up and tied back, which gave the sandal a graceful appearance. At times sides were added to the base, creating a type of footwear that was still a sandal, not quite an enclosed shoe. Occasionally sandals made of gold sheet have been found in royal burials, and others made of wood come from private tombs, but it is very doubtful that these were truly used in life.

JEWELRY

One of the most appealing aspects of Egyptian dress and costume results from the apparent widespread love of brightly colored jewelry. Cyril Aldred, an Egyptologist who made a special study of the subject, believed that most Egyptian jewelry was amuletic, or meant to magically protect the wearer. He came to this conclusion because much of the jewelry was formed with images of the gods, sacred animals, or other designs that suggested power or security; jewelry was almost always meant to be a safeguard against disease, accident, and other misfortune. Certainly the amuletic aspect of Egyptian jewelry was incorporated into and dictated much of the design.

Whatever the underlying reasons, the ancient Egyptians were obviously fond of personal adornment in the form of jewelry. This may also have been influenced by the general lack of color in clothing. In any case, there was an exceptional variety of types of jewelry used and enjoyed by the Egyptians. The long list of decorative types includes hair bands, diadems and crowns, as well as hairpins, earrings, necklaces, beaded collars, pendants or pectorals, belts or circlets, bracelets, armlets, anklets, and finger rings. In short, almost every exposed part of the body would eventually have some kind of decoration.

The materials employed in jewelry making were extremely varied. The metals included copper, gold, silver, and electrum, an alloy of gold and silver. Many different natural stones, such as quartzite, carnelian, lapis lazuli, turquoise, and hematite, were popularly used. The turquoise came mainly from mines in the nearby Sinai peninsula, but the lapis lazuli, a deep-blue-colored mineral, had to be imported from faraway Afghanistan. Additional stones and minerals found in Egyptian jewelry include amethyst, chalcedony, feldspar, red garnet, jasper, obsidian, and steatite. Artificial and composite substances such as Egyptian faience and glass supplemented all of these natural materials. It should be pointed out that the gemstones considered most valuable today – diamond, ruby, and emerald – were unknown to the Egyptians, and the materials used in ancient jewelry were chosen as much for the symbolism of their colors as for any decorative effect or presumed rarity.

In addition to the jewelry made of costly material for the elite, a range of simple jewelry was available to the less affluent. Animal bones and seashells were readily available and could be easily worked into designs by cutting and engraving. Tortoise and oyster shell, cowry, mother of pearl, and even ostrich eggshell were also used. The source of animal bones is self-evident; the seashells were obtained from the Mediterranean and the Red Sea and perhaps as fossils from the natural limestone layers of the hills. The form of the cowry shell was so popular for sexually symbolic reasons that it was copied in gold for the wealthy. Gold cowry shells were strung into belts or girdles and sometimes contained hard pellets of stone or metal meant to rattle or jangle when the wearer moved.

The history of the desire for bodily adornment is attested early in Egyptian history. Beads from the Predynastic Period show that clearly. The glazed beads found in Predynastic burials are simple, but they already demonstrate the technological advances that enabled the early Egyptian to pierce a piece of stone and coat it with a shiny-colored surface. It was probably an accidental discovery that a combination of silica (from crushed sand) and soda (found naturally in the desert), when heated, could form a glasslike material. This discovery led later to the use of the substance in a range of forms, discussed in the chapter on glass and Egyptian faience.

In the Predynastic Period, in addition to glazed beads, a number of natural colored stones were already in use, including turquoise, carnelian, and jasper. Shell, ivory, and bone supplemented this choice of decorative materials. Choices were made for their color and for magical associations, based on perceived similarities and sympathetic magic. For example, the red of carnelian resembled the red of blood, and blood implied life, strength, and vigor. The symbolic association of colors became more complex as time passed and became part of the vocabulary of amulets. As early as the Predynastic Period these decorative/protective objects began to be made in a wide variety of forms, resembling the charms on a modern bracelet, but with far more significance. These amulets were worn partly as decoration but were considered protection against all manner of serious life-threatening situations, including illness and accident.

In the beginnings of the Dynastic Period, when the country was first unified under one ruler, the arts and crafts began to flourish in the service of both royal and private patrons. In addition to the necklaces of simple strings of beads, the wide beaded collar and elaborate bracelets became popular. Among the earliest examples of more complex jewelry that have been preserved is a group of bracelets of King Djer, of Dynasty One. The materials of four bracelets include gold, turquoise, lapis lazuli, and amethyst. They show not only the interest in rare, exotic, and valuable substances but also the high level of craftsmanship developed early in Egyptian history. One of the bracelets consists of twenty-seven alternating plaques of gold and turquoise shaped like *serekhs*. The *serekh* is a hieroglyphic device in the shape of a palace façade with the falcon of the god Horus on its top. This was the customary design used to enclose the name of the king in early times, and its use continued through history for the writing of one of his several names as the king's titles became more complicated. The bracelets of King Djer not only tell us about the state of the crafts but are also evidence of the emergence of the jewelry maker as a specialized craftsman.

It is obvious that our knowledge of ancient jewelry is dependent on accidents of preservation and discovery, as it is with almost every other aspect of life in ancient Egypt. It is also clear that for the history of early jewelry most of the evidence comes from royal or upper class burials. The tomb prepared for Queen Hetepheres, the mother of King Khufu, builder of the Great Pyramid, represents one such happy accident. Near the foot of her son's monument a small shaft tomb was discovered. Among the remains were traces of jewelry boxes that had once contained personal ornaments of the queen. These included a large set of matched silver bracelets. The wooden boxes had disintegrated and the silver was badly corroded, but when the bracelets were cleaned it was seen that they had butterfly designs inlaid in colored stone of carnelian, lapis lazuli, and turquoise. These rare, preserved examples of Old Kingdom jewelry demonstrate that colorful designs were prized by royalty and the elite and that the technology of metalworking and inlay had reached a high level early in Egyptian history. This love of rich adornment and body decoration never ended in ancient Egypt.

A contrasting example to the royal chance discovery was the find of a simple burial in a humble grave at the site of Mendes, in the eastern Nile delta. It was not a preserved mummy and the individual so buried was probably not of sufficient rank to afford mummification, but he had around his neck a single gold wire with a few stone beads. This single bit of gold suggests that the person received some sort of reward or distinction in life that became his prized treasure to take to the grave.

Probably the most typical jewelry form throughout Egyptian history was the wide beaded collar (called *wesekh* in ancient Egyptian). One Egyptologist called beads the "building blocks" of jewelry because they were so often used in many different ways and could be assembled in so many different forms. The wide semicircular collar was one of the most popular and long lasting of these forms. In addition to actual examples that have been found, this type of collar is often shown in painting and sculpture, worn by men and women alike. The beads from which it was made could be mainly blue, from the copper compound used to color the faience material, or multicolored in imitation of flower petals. The wide collar was usually attached to a counterweight that hung down the person's back and served to keep the collar in place. It is believed that the "floral" collars of the New Kingdom were based on collars really made of papyrus and flowers. Examples of these have been found where the once fresh flowers were interwoven into a backing of papyrus that provided the general form. When new, these must have been an attractive (and fragrant) addition to the costume of the wearer.

The common use of wigs dictated that some sort of hair band was needed to keep them in place, so a range of circlets or diadems was devised. In some cases these hair bands were made of silver or gold decorated with colored stone inlays. Others were made of multiple strings of beads that served the same purpose. The more elaborate were usually decorated with floral designs in imitation of a wreathlike headdress made of flowers. In some inscriptions this kind of headdress is called a "boatman's circlet," harking back to those made of lilies and papyrus shown on the heads of boatmen in Old Kingdom relief carvings. In many examples of ancient Egyptian decoration the design of elements used in objects of adornment can be traced back to natural plant and animal forms commonly found in the land.

Earrings as a class of jewelry do not make a general appearance in Egypt until the New Kingdom, and it is possible that the custom of wearing earrings was introduced during the incursions of foreigners in the Second Intermediate Period. The design of earrings ranged from a simple ring to extremely complex and bulky objects that were of such a weight that they doubtless distended the ear lobes. In addition to rings for the ears, there were also ear studs of various designs ranging from a mushroom-shaped glass object to a type with two domed heads joined by a screw shank. The size of the earring post and studs could be roughly the diameter of a modern pencil, suggesting that the earlobe had to be gradually stretched to accommodate the size of the object. In addition to ear studs there were also disk-shaped decorations about the size of a silver dollar, fashioned with a groove around the diameter. Because of their size they have often been identified or described as spools, bobbins, or even gaming pieces, but they were intended to fit in an earlobe that had been gradually lengthened to accommodate them. Some mummies have been found with distended earlobes of this shape that prove this idea.

One of the favorite types of jewelry for royalty and the elite class was the pectoral, or large and elaborate pendant worn hanging on the chest. From Tutankhamun's tomb and from some other burials of royal family members have come a number of examples of such large decorations. Typically they are made of a gold body inlaid with semiprecious stones in elaborate designs. The nature of these designs, usually of a complex symbolism, suggests that they were for special ceremonial use and were not only body embellishments that incorporated religious ideas. These were often described in the past as made of paste enamel inlays (cloisonné), but close inspection often indicates that the metal body of the object, the matrix, was fashioned with shaped depressions to receive the bits of stone that were carefully and laboriously cut to fit.

The Egyptians virtually invented the finger ring as a body decoration and its use can be attested as early as the Predynastic Period. Rings appear in a range of forms, from a simple band, even a knotted string with an amulet attached, to the weighty jeweled treasures of kings. The material of which rings were made ranged from gold, silver, and electrum to Egyptian faience. The elaborate and costly examples almost always have a series of amuletic symbols or an abbreviated prayer or invocation to a god. By contrast simple faience rings have been found that are plain unadorned circles, while others were made with a bezel incorporating a single device such as the Eye of Horus or a simple representation of a god or gods.

An examination of the range of jewelry in ancient Egypt is completed with belts or circlets, bracelets, armlets, and anklets. The belts were of flexible beading or, as previously described, occasionally were made with cowry shell shapes interspersed with beading. Bracelets could also be constructed of flexible beading, as were armlets for the upper arm and anklets. The designs of bracelets could incorporate colored semiprecious stones fashioned in symbolic shapes.

With the large range of jewelry types that have been preserved by chance, it is still important to remember that many examples come from noble and even royal contexts and often do not represent either the adornments of the ordinary people or even the everyday wear of the upper classes. The average working-class person could not afford expensive jewelry, whereas royalty and the elite chose to display their wealth as conspicuous symbols of their rank or station. Nevertheless, there were opportunities for those who were not wealthy and privileged to enjoy some forms of jewelry. Amulets and decorative devices could be made of Egyptian faience in endless duplicates from molds made of stone or clay. Faience beads were

FIGURE 24   **Gable-topped chest and linens. New Kingdom**
Clothing was stored in baskets or chests such as this one. This typical storage box
with lid contains a shirt, or tunic, and other linens.
The Metropolitan Museum of Art, Rogers Fund, 1936 (36.3.54, 36.3.56a, b, 36.3.111,
36.3.140) (36.3.54, 36.3.56a, b, 36.3.111, 36.3.140). Reproduction of any kind is prohibited without express written permission in advance from the Metropolitan
Museum of Art.

simple to produce as well and were probably the most universal form
of decoration. As suggested earlier, shell and bone could be fashioned in a variety of ways to fill the need for less expensive forms of
jewelry. In any case, the love of colorful body decoration seems to
have been a part of life, whatever the rank of the individual.

After examination of dress, hairstyles, footwear, jewelry, and
other costume considerations it is possible to say that nowhere else
in the ancient world has provided us with such an abundance of
preserved information concerning how people dressed and what
they believed to be attractive bodily adornment. The combination
of artistic representations and actual objects presents a detailed and
varied panorama of cultural images spanning a range from the formal garments of royalty to the loincloth of the field worker. Always
being aware of the functional restrictions of Egyptian art and the
symbolic nature of what is represented, it is still possible to gain
considerable knowledge of the way many classes of Egyptians were
clothed and the way costume styles evolved over three thousand
years (Fig. 24).

Aldred, C. *Jewels of the Pharaohs.* London: Praeger, 1971.
Dayagi-Mendels, Michal. *Perfumes and Cosmetics in the Ancient
World.* The Israel Museum, 1989.

Hall, Rosalind M. "Garments in the Petrie Museum of Archaeology." *Textile History* 13 (1), 27–45, 1982.

Egyptian Textiles. Aylesbury: Shire Egyptology, 1986.

Vogelsang-Eastwood, Gillian. *Patterns for Ancient Egyptian Clothing.* Publisher not given, undated.

Pharaonic Egyptian Clothing. Leiden: E. J. Brill, 1993.

"Textiles" in *Ancient Egyptian Materials and Technology*, edited by Paul T. Nicholson and Ian Shaw. Cambridge: Cambridge University Press, 2000. Pp. 268–298.

5

Housing and Furniture

Making furniture in ivory and ebony, in sesnedjem wood and meru wood, in real cedar from the heights of the terraced hills ...

FROM THE TOMB OF REKHMIRE IN THEBES

In ancient Egypt there was a clear distinction between the architecture of temples and tombs in contrast with the structures for the living. Temples and tombs, the houses of the gods and the eternal homes for the spirits, were made of durable stone. Palaces for royalty and houses for all levels of society were made of much more perishable stuff. For practical use the principal building material of the ancient Egyptians was sun-dried, unbaked brick made of Nile mud. This cannot be emphasized too strongly for an understanding of living conditions in ancient Egypt. In the contemporary United States this use of material can best be compared to the use of mud brick in the adobe structures of the American southwest, although mud brick is still an important building material in many other parts of the world.

Mud brick is a practical material that requires only a minimum amount of skill to produce. In ancient Egypt the bricks were formed in a wooden mold using earth mixed with water, perhaps with the addition of chopped straw or other natural materials to act as a binder. They were then laid out in rows to dry in the sun and cure to a degree of hardness suitable for construction. Actual preserved examples of the wooden brick molds have been found. Depictions on tomb walls, particularly in the Theban tomb of Rekhmire, show the process exactly as it is still carried out in Egypt today (Fig. 25).

The rooms in most houses were necessarily small due to the lack of abundant timber of a size and strength capable of spanning large spaces for roofing or upper flooring. Where a larger space was desired a center post or column to help support the roof or upper stories was used. Floors were made of hard pounded earth that was sometimes plastered. Interior walls were also usually plastered and could be enhanced with painted decoration. The plaster of the walls was renewed occasionally to counter the effects of wear or damage,

FIGURE 25   Painting illustrating the making of mud brick
Theban Tomb 100, tomb of Rekhmire
Unbaked mud brick was the chief building material for domestic
structures. The steps in the production are shown: mixing the earth
and water, using a wooden mold to form the bricks, and laying out
the bricks to dry in the sun.
Author's photograph

and this custom of renewal can clearly be seen in the multiple layers
of plaster found on the remains of excavated walls. The thickness
required of mud brick walls in construction provided a natural insu-
lation that made the structure cooler in summer and retained heat in
winter. If contemporary mud brick houses in Egypt can be used as a
comparison, the result was a pleasant, comfortable, and clean dwelling, naturally depending on care and upkeep.

One additional advantage of mud brick construction was the ease
with which a structure could be altered and expanded, repaired, or
even completely destroyed to make way for new building. When a
house or other structure no longer served a useful purpose it could
be completely razed and the brick broken up to level the ground for a
new construction. This method of reuse of a site is part of the explanation for the villages that seem to be built on mounds called *koms*
or *tells*, common in the Near East and Egypt. Because the remains of
many succeeding layers of dwellings have accumulated from rebuild-
ing on the same location, they have created hill-like structures that
rise up from the level plain. Archaeological investigation of such
mounds can often reveal a complex series of successive habitation
layers that span generations and even centuries.

FIGURE 26   An ancient Egyptian model of a house. Third Intermediate or Greco-Roman Period
The three stories are clearly shown as well as some material stowed on the roof. Although many dwellings were only a single story, this model attests to the existence of more elaborate houses. Some remains of two- and three-story ancient mud brick houses also still exist in Egypt today.
Photograph © The Trustees of the British Museum

There are numerous diagrammatic representations of houses and estates painted on the walls of tombs, and there are also a number of models (sometimes called "soul houses") that were made to be included in tombs to be useful to the spirit of the dead. The paintings and models both show that houses could be two and sometimes three stories high, with the upper levels reached by stairs or ladders (Fig. 26). Evidence for multistoried houses also exists on several archaeological sites, including the remains of the Coptic/Byzantine community within the precincts of the Temple of Medinet Habu, in Thebes, and those of the town of Tell Timai, in the eastern delta.

One of the most important assets of the mud brick structure was the roof. It was often treated as an additional living space, like a terrace, where the dwellers could find some relief from the summer heat. One type of roof top feature that is sometimes illustrated in

FIGURE 27   **Remains of houses. New Kingdom**
Deir el Medina, the workmen's village, with the tombs of the villag-
ers in the distance. The walls were built partly of limestone in addition to the mud brick, probably accounting for their preservation.
Author's photograph

wall paintings is a kind of air scoop, designed to catch the cool wind
from the north and direct it down into the house. This arrangement
persisted into recent times and can still be seen in photographs of
nineteenth-century Cairo. This could have been an important asset
because windows were not a common feature of most houses. The
idea of being able to see out through windows does not seem to have
been an ancient Egyptian preference except in dwellings of more
than one story. This was partly for security and partly a product of
the lack of technology for glazing or otherwise closing windows.
Where windows were used on upper levels they could be closed
with mats or shades.

The level of complexity in the layout of an Egyptian house was
directly dependent on the social status and wealth of the owner. On
the simplest level a dwelling would usually consist of only two or
three rooms (Fig. 27). Cooking and sanitary solutions were accomplished out of doors for the most part. More elaborate houses of
the elite were naturally larger and more complex, with kitchens,
lavatories, interior courtyards, pools, and even gardens. In the models made for the tomb of the high official Meketre there are two
examples included that reproduced the appearance of interior courts

FIGURE 28   Model of a garden and portico. Dynasty Eleven
Theban Tomb 280, the tomb of Meketre.
A garden was an important part of the complex houses of the affluent. It provided
an area of vegetation and color in an enclosed dwelling that looked in on itself.
The Metropolitan Museum of Art, Rogers Fund and Edward S. Harkness Gift, 1920
(20.3.13). Reproduction of any kind is prohibited without express written permission in advance from the Metropolitan Museum of Art.

or gardens complete with miniature trees (Fig. 28). The models are
even furnished with copper basins to hold the water for the pools, to
complete the image of a pleasant retreat. These models underscore
the importance of such amenities in the life of those who could
afford them. The central court with gardens and pools made a pleasant contrast to the outside world and shut out the noise and activity
of the outside (Fig. 29).

In the modern world, because it seems a natural solution, we give
little thought to why most cities are laid out in intersecting streets
on a practical rectangular grid pattern of right angles, or how that
may have come about. This kind of organization is not always true
of the old cities of the Middle East and Europe because many of
them were not purposefully planned but grew and expanded in a

FIGURE 29   Painting of a garden with a T-shaped pool and grape arbor. Dynasty
Eighteen
Theban Tomb 90, tomb of Nebamun
In the houses of the affluent enclosed gardens and arbors were
often used for contrasting space to the small, windowless rooms.
Author's photograph

haphazard manner. Streets turn and wander, intersecting each other
at strange angles and creating odd shapes and spaces. In order to have
logical relationships of streets and spaces, villages and towns require
forethought and planning. The earliest examples of "city planning"
that we can recognize in ancient Egypt are found in the cities for
the dead, such as the necropolis at Giza around the three pyramids
of Dynasty Four. At that site the tombs are laid out on intersecting
streets in a grid pattern. Even though this plan was meant for tombs
and not dwellings for the living, it is an indication that the ideal
arrangement for houses could be a logical and orderly one.

A further example of planning is proved by the remains of a temporary village at Lahun, near the Fayum, that was built for workmen
and overseers who labored on the construction of a Middle Kingdom
pyramid. This self-contained site was intended to be abandoned after
the construction project was finished. However the ground plan is preserved and it serves as an excellent example of a planned community.
A much more elaborate city plan was developed for the new capital
founded by the Pharoah Akhenaten as his new home and the principal
site of his worship of the sun god. In the case of Akhenaten's ideal city,
a regular grid plan was laid out in the early stage of planning; the main
areas adhered to the plan, but the outlying parts did not.

In contrast to regular planning, the village of Deir el Medina,
on the west bank at Thebes, was organized around only a few main

FIGURE 30   **Remains of houses at Deir el Medina. New Kingdom**
In the workmen's village the remains clearly show the long, narrow layout of the dwellings. Although the workmen who lived there were of a special class, the type of house plan was probably typical.
Author's photograph

streets and shows clear signs of growth and expansion over time (Fig. 30). As such, it represents a more typical type of village layout that had no overall plan at its beginnings and grew to meet an expanding population. Deir el Medina is an unusual case in that it was the home of the craftsmen and artisans who labored in the excavation and decoration of the royal tombs in the Valley of the Kings and Queens. The inhabitants were high-level specialized professionals whose living arrangements do not completely represent those of typical laborers. Nevertheless, the information to be gained from the remains of Deir el Medina is valuable for some understanding of house design and living arrangements for some of the working classes.

FURNITURE

A wide variety of furniture types and styles is attested throughout Egyptian history, but it is a common mistake to imagine that all classes had household furnishings made of wood available to them. Furniture-quality wood was accessible only in limited quantities and was therefore rare and expensive. In fact, much of it had to be imported. Most of the evidence for furniture making comes from the tombs of the upper classes and gives a picture of how the well-to-do lived, but it tells us little or nothing about the household furnishings of other levels. There are virtually no clues preserved as to how an ordinary laborer would have furnished his simple dwelling. The reasonable conclusion to be reached is that he and his family probably sat and slept on mats on the floor. The material from the workmen's village at Deir el Medina, where the homes were those of skilled craftsmen, represents a different situation. At Deir el Medina workmen's families possessed limited amounts of furniture, but it was of simple design and construction, much simpler than the examples found in tombs of the higher classes. Some of the workmen there even engaged in the production of furniture during periods when they were not working on tomb projects.

It is obvious that people of wealth and privilege had the resources to furnish their houses and villas with furniture carefully crafted, often of exotic materials such as ebony and ivory. Stools and mats and objects made of woven reed and rattan were probably the extent of furnishings for the lower ranks. However, the basic types of furniture that have been preserved were very much what we still use today – chairs, stools, tables, stands, beds, and chests (Fig. 31). In addition to these basic items there was one type of object not much used in Western cultures. This was the headrest, apparently a standard necessity for sleeping arrangements.

It is fortunate that there are sufficient examples of furniture that have been found in tombs that illustrate all of the most typical forms as well as demonstrate the skill of the furniture maker or joiner (Fig. 32). To supplement the actual objects there are meticulous illustrations of many of the activities of furniture production in paintings and relief carvings, often rendered in great detail. Craftsmen are shown in every stage of the work, from splitting planks (Fig. 33) in the rough preparation of the wood to the fine carving of furniture parts and the drilling of holes in beds and chairs for the lacing that would provide a flexible resting surface.

FIGURE 31   Funerary procession with some of the basic types of furniture. Dynasty Eighteen
Theban Tomb 55, tomb of Ramose
On the right, a chair; in the center, a group of boxes; to the left, a bed with head-
rest; and below that, a stool: all are typical examples of Egyptian furniture.
Author's photograph

FIGURE 32   A group of furniture pieces. Various dates
These include a three-legged table, a low chair, and a stool (missing its lacing
seat). These show a range of craftsmanship, from very high in the case of the chair,
with its elaborately carved back, to the simple, almost crude workmanship of the
table.
Photograph © The Trustees of the British Museum

FIGURE 33   Carpenter splitting planks. Dynasty Eighteen
Theban Tomb 181, tomb of Nebamun and Ipuki
The Egyptian carpenter and furniture maker was necessarily skilled
in every step, from the preparation of the raw material to the accomplishment of finished detail. In the absence of metal aids such as
vises, binding with rope had to suffice to hold the work.
Drawing by the author after figure 25 in *Egypt's Golden Age*

In the range of materials employed for furniture, wood was
the most common, but ivory, metal, wickerwork, and even stone
were used. Among the woods were the native sycamore fig, acacia, and tamarisk, and the imported hardwoods including cedar,
juniper, and ebony. The limited range of hand tools employed for
woodworking included the axe, adze, saw, chisel, and bow drill,
which are further discussed in the chapter on tools and weapons.
For working with wood the Egyptians developed the mortise and
tenon joint early in Dynastic history as well as a variety of miter
joints for the corners of boxes and coffins. Joins were strengthened
at first by lashing with leather strips, but over time this method
was eventually replaced by the use of wooden pegs and some types
of gluing and clamping. Other very sophisticated techniques of
woodworking were eventually developed, including the use of
laminated plywood and the bending and shaping of wood with
heat or moisture to create curved and rounded surfaces. Very little

metal was used in the production of furniture except for large staples used for the lashing that secured the lids of boxes and the door of chests.

Whereas wood was the material used for more substantial furniture, rattan work made from reeds and rushes was often employed for boxes and chests as well as for lightweight stands or tables, stools, and even chairs. Boxes for the storage of wigs were often made of this material. Rattan work became especially popular in the New Kingdom, when the techniques of manipulating the materials were taken to a high state of development.

Styles of furniture changed significantly during the Old Kingdom, as did almost every other aspect of Egyptian life. King Djoser, in Dynasty Three, is depicted in sculpture as seated on a throne that is represented as if it were made of undecorated slabs of wood, presenting almost a basic diagram of a chair. By the time of King Khafre, in Dynasty Four, the royal throne is represented in sculpture as a carefully rendered chair type that becomes very familiar as a traditional Egyptian design. This furniture style uses imitations of animal parts, fore and hind legs, for the chair legs. However, this use of animal legs with claw or hoof was not a new innovation in Dynasty Four. Some examples of furniture parts done in this type of stylization, even carved from a rare material such as ivory, have been recovered from graves and tombs of the Predynastic and Early Dynastic periods. These earlier examples of furniture legs are short and squat and seem to have been intended for beds or, more likely, for small tables or gaming boards, rather than for chairs.

In the fully developed style of Dynasty Four, the leg elements are carefully designed with great attention to the anatomical details of animal parts. The two main types represented have either the paw of a feline or the sharp hoof of a horned animal, but both are usually supported on a small cone-shaped pedestal. It is particularly interesting that a style originating with the ancient Egyptians that featured furniture legs ending in an animal's claw has continued to appear in furniture for more than five thousand years.

There are few actual examples of Old Kingdom furniture that have been preserved, but fortunately there are many depictions of furniture in tomb decoration from this period. The paintings in the tomb of an official named Hesire, who lived during the reign of Djoser, provide us with a virtual catalog of furniture types used during Dynasty Three. These paintings are among the earliest graphic examples to contain such variety and detail, and they add to our knowledge of furniture design during the first stages in Egyptian history. Among the objects represented are beds, chairs, tables, several types of stools, boxes, and even the parts of a portable kiosk or canopy. The beds and stools are delineated in great detail to illustrate the methods of attaching leg elements and even the lacing of the sleeping surfaces. The many types of personal possessions and equipment that the boxes were meant to contain are depicted beside or above them. This served to create a visual inventory that ranges from tools and clothing to the ever-present headrests.

A group of furniture pieces from the tomb of Hetepheres, the mother of King Khufu, provides rare evidence of actual Old Kingdom furniture. In the section on personal adornment we have previously mentioned some of her jewelry. The discovery of these royal objects is a particularly interesting episode in the history of archaeology. At Giza, near the Great Pyramid, an American expedition under the direction of Egyptologist George Andrew Reisner found a small tomb chamber at the bottom of a shaft cut deep in the limestone plateau. In addition to a stone sarcophagus, there were the remains of several objects including a chair, bed, and a litter or carrying chair, with a group of poles for the supports for a portable canopy (like the ones pictured in the tomb of Hesire). The wooden parts of these objects had long ago disintegrated, but the gold tube sheeting that had covered them was intact enough to provide the careful excavators with information so that the objects could be fully reconstructed. As a product of their painstaking archaeological work it was possible to recover the appearance of these extraordinary examples of royal furniture from the beginning of Dynasty Four.

The style of Hetepheres' furniture was simple, clean, and sparingly decorated. The essential structural elements were not disguised by ornate or elaborate embellishments, as sometimes found in later New Kingdom furniture. The basic shapes were rectangular and cubic. In addition to the gold coverings, the simple decorative elements used include legs of chairs and beds in animal shapes and palm-shaped terminals on the handles of the carrying chair. This last object was also decorated on the back of the seat with an inlay bearing the name and titles of its owner, as was the box for the canopy parts. In pictorial representations from Dynasties Four and Five, furniture used by the nobility is often depicted with the same simplicity and spare style as the royal furniture. Where carrying chairs are shown they follow the same straightforward pattern as that of Hetepheres. The animal leg elements in furniture persisted, however.

Chairs continued to be made in the simple, square pattern of Hetepheres' furniture, both with and without arms. However, the

FIGURE 34   Chair of Renyseneb. Dynasty Eighteen
This well-preserved piece of furniture clearly shows the characteristics of an Egyptian chair with legs that end in feline paws and a seat of woven webbing. The use of ebony and ivory indicates that it was intended for the use of a well-to-do individual.
The Metropolitan Museum of Art, Rogers Fund and Edward S. Harkness Gift, 1920 (20.3.13). Reproduction of any kind is prohibited without express written permission in advance from the Metropolitan Museum of Art.

more elaborate and decorative style with animal legs increasingly became the norm for the elite, and there are numerous examples preserved as well as depicted (Fig. 34). In the New Kingdom, as exemplified by the furniture of Tutankhamun, chairs, especially those for ceremonial purposes, became highly decorated with the imported ebony and ivory inlay. Improvement in structural stability was made in the New Kingdom when a vertical brace was added to the slightly sloping back.

To judge from the many examples of stools that have been found preserved in tombs, they were by far the most common piece of furniture used by the Egyptians, in contrast to elaborately worked chairs (Fig. 35). Stools are commonly lower than chairs and by definition obviously have no backrest. Stools could be made with four legs, a slightly curved seat, and latticework bracing, or, at their most simple, with three legs with a solid, flat, wooden slab seat. A special

FIGURE 35   **Wooden stool. Dynasty Eighteen**
The stool was probably the most useful piece of furniture for all classes.
The elaborate cross bracing in this example gave extra strength, and
the concave top provided space for a pillow or padding.
Photograph © The Trustees of the British Museum

type of folding stool was designed with crossed legs and a leather or
fabric seat. One of the distinctive features of most folding stools was
the use of duck or goose heads to form the shape of the lower end of
the leg. These stools were certainly portable and probably suitable
for travel.

Beds were constructed as a simple frame standing on short legs
with a network of lacing to support a mattress pad of folded linen.
The typical bed sloped down from head to foot, ending in a vertical
footboard. The frame was drilled with a series of holes to accommodate the cross lacing that provided the sleeping surface. This repeated
drilling was accomplished with a bow drill, often illustrated in tomb
paintings of carpenters at work. Examples of beds have been found
with and without their original lacing, which was fragile and more
susceptible to decay. The footboard was probably intended to keep
the sleeper from slipping too far down on the simple bed. Since it

FIGURE 36   Workmen carrying a bed and cloths. Old Kingdom
After Lepsius, *Denkmaeler*, Vol. 2, plate 6
The bed shown is unusual in that it has no footboard, but it does have curved
bracing made of bent wood members. The accompanying servant is carrying the
linen cloth that would provide the needed padding.
Drawing by the author

is more common in modern cultures to have a raised headboard
rather than one at the foot, people often misunderstand the design of
Egyptian beds, where the reverse is true. From the evidence found
in some tombs the bed was completed with folded linen sheets as
padding, which served at a thin mattress (Fig. 36).

A piece of furniture related to the bed is the back rest, an object
that looks very much like a sloping bed with only one pair of legs. It
is mainly known from representations in tombs and not from actual
examples. What its purpose was and when it was used is still a mystery, but it seems to have been popular in the Old Kingdom. Another
unusual example of sleeping accommodation is the so-called camp
bed found in the tomb of Tutankhamun. It was apparently designed
for traveling, because it was hinged in two places so that it could be
folded to a third of its length.

Most Egyptian beds are of simple design, little more than a modern cot, and one should not confuse beds for daily use with others that were employed only for funeral purposes. There are three
examples of these special beds from the Tutankhamun tomb. They
are much taller than ordinary beds and have decoration relating to
the funerary ritual in which they were used.

One of the unusual objects of furniture preserved from ancient Egypt is the headrest. It is different from almost anything used in modern times but it was an important accessory to the Egyptian bed as a substitute for a soft pillow for sleeping in ancient times. It is true that pillows were used as cushions on chairs and even on balustrades, for leaning, but they are seen only occasionally as a part of sleeping equipment. Headrests look as if they would provide an uncomfortable surface to rest on, but they were so widely used that in one tomb decoration five different styles of headrests are shown.

The basic headrest was a T-shaped object that consisted of a wide base and a slightly concave top supported on a post that was five or six inches high. If a person slept on one side, the headrest made up for the width of the shoulder. Small statuettes of women sleeping with a headrest always show them resting on one side. Headrests were made of a variety of materials, but the practical ones were usually of wood. Some that have been found in tombs are made of alabaster or limestone and were probably symbolic and not used in life. Tutankhamun even had one headrest made of cast glass, which was certainly too fragile to have been a functional example. The typical shape of the headrest was reproduced as an amulet, probably having to do with the concept of "raising the head," or resurrection.

In reliefs that depict the funerary offerings, another type of furniture often represented is a small round table like a tray with a pedestal. This object seems to have had limited use for special purposes. It was made of stone and is often depicted as supported and elevated on a nearly cylindrical stand. Without the stand it would have been suitable for use by people who were seated on the floor or on low stools. With the addition of the stand it was raised to the convenient height for someone seated on a full-sized chair, as it is when included in the standard scenes of funerary offerings.

The type of table more often represented is made of wood, with a rectangular top and four legs. Fortunately a number of actual examples of wooden tables have been preserved. They are usually of simple design, with plain, straight legs, unlike the chairs or beds with animal legs. A design innovation introduced in the New Kingdom made it usual to strengthen furniture with "stretchers," the horizontal cross bracing that served to keep the legs from spreading. In some examples this strengthening is further accomplished with the use of a bent wood brace that curves at the joint between leg and table or chair seat. The design of tables with strictly vertical legs was gradually supplanted in the New Kingdom by one with slightly slanting legs. This type has a resemblance to the shape of a temple

FIGURE 37   **Basket, box, and jar. New Kingdom**
The covered basket, jewelry box with sliding lid, and alabaster cosmetics jar demonstrate three main types of storage containers, each designed for its special
purpose.
The Metropolitan Museum of Art, Rogers Fund, 1936 (36.3.189a, b, 36.3.190a–c,
36.3.199) (36.3.189a, b, 36.3.190a–c, 36.3.199). Reproduction of any kind is prohibited without express written permission in advance from the Metropolitan
Museum of Art.

pylon or shrine, even to the out-turned cornice below the top surface. In addition to those made of wood, tables were also made of
wickerwork with elaborate cross bracing. In wooden tables some
of the cross bracing seems to be a holdover as imitation from those
made of wicker.

  The safe storage of clothing, wigs, jewelry, cosmetics, and other
personal items presented an important problem for people who lived
in mud brick houses. For most the problems were solved with boxes,
chests, and baskets, rather than with elaborate pieces of furniture
such as the modern chests of drawers (Fig. 37). Fortunately, there
are numerous depictions of chests and boxes in tomb decoration,
and there are a number of preserved examples as well. The Egyptian

chest was usually a cubic shape with either a sliding lid or a lid that was separate but fitted. Hinges did not seem to play an important functional part in chest design. The overall shapes varied in having flat, gabled, or curved roofs, and the contents could be secured by tying cords around two knobs, one on the lid and one on the side of the container. Sometimes chests were designed with short legs and retractable poles so they that could be carried by two bearers like a modern stretcher. Chests were very versatile and could be adapted for the storage needs of the particular owner. The interior could sometimes be fitted or divided into compartments to accommodate the types of objects the chest was meant to contain.

The importance of chests for storage is illustrated in the depictions of funeral processions where the furniture for the tomb is included. There are usually several people bearing chests that undoubtedly were meant to contain clothing and other personal items. However, baskets fitted with their own covers also played an important storage role and were probably more often employed because the materials for basketmaking were readily available and economical, unlike wood, which was scarce and often expensive.

The two principal lighting methods available to the ancient Egyptians were lamps and torches. In almost all periods the Egyptian lamp was a simple device consisting of a floating wick in a shallow dish of oil or animal fat. The wick was often a twist of linen fabric; the oil was derived from vegetable sources such as olive or sesame, and the fat from a variety of animals. Lamps could be placed on the floor, elevated on a cylindrical lampstand, or placed in a niche in the wall. Egyptian lamps fueled by oil or animal fat probably gave very little light, but in a society where life was regulated by the cycle of the sun, where people rose with the sunrise and rested at nightfall, there was not a great deal of dependence on artificial lighting. In recent years, before the general electrification of the country resulting from the dam at Aswan, it was possible to enter a rural village in Egypt that seemed to be in total darkness. After a period of adjustment it could become possible to see that the inhabitants were sitting in front of their houses or going about their tasks because they were accustomed to the lack of artificial light. This experience comes close to suggesting what darkness meant to the ancient Egyptians and how even the simplest lamp would have been of great benefit.

One special situation that did require some method of extra light was for the work in the excavation of tombs. Obviously light was required for the workmen who carved out the interior spaces and decorated the tombs of royalty and nobility. There has been some question as to whether those laborers used lamps, torches, or even some method of reflecting sunlight into the dark interiors. It was probably some combination of the three, but a definitive answer has not been found.

For most ancient Egyptians the design of furniture continued to be relatively simple over three thousand years, each basic type suited by necessity to its particular use. Except for the overly ornate examples made for royalty, where it was considered appropriate to incorporate symbolic images or designs for ritual purposes, it was not always considered important to embellish furniture to a great extent with decorative patterns or inscriptions. The limited materials of furniture quality available were utilized in ingenious ways in the construction of sturdy and durable household furnishings. As in every other part of life among the ancient Egyptians, the amount and kind of furnishings depended on the class and occupation of the owner. Since the actual examples of furniture and the representations in tombs reflect the taste and affluence of the privileged class, our knowledge is necessarily limited and obviously does not reflect the needs of the vast majority of the population. However, there are a number of plain, unadorned chairs, tables, and stools that have been preserved. These serve as a kind of middle ground between the furnishings of the well-to-do and those of the poorest classes and help to make a more complete picture of the furniture craft.

Arnold, Dieter. *Building in Egypt: Pharaonic Stone Masonry*. New York: Oxford University Press, 1991.

Baker, Hollis S. *Furniture in the Ancient World*. New York: Giniger/MacMillan, 1965.

Kemp, Barry. "Soil (including mud brick architecture)" in *Ancient Egyptian Materials and Technology*, edited by Paul T. Nicholson and Ian Shaw. Cambridge: Cambridge University Press, 2000. Pp. 78–103.

Killen, Geoffrey. *Egyptian Woodworking and Furniture*. Aylesbury: Shire Egyptology, 1994.

Spencer, A. J. *Brick Architecture in Ancient Egypt*. Warminster: Aris and Phillips, 1979.

Food and Drink

6

On that day the workman Menna gave the pot of fresh fat to the chief of the
Medjay [police] Mentmose who said "I will pay you for it with barley."

MEMORANDUM OF PAYMENT OWED

One of the most important and characteristic aspects of any civilization is the way that people were able to nourish themselves, the kinds of food and drink that were available to them. In a culture with the geographical advantages of ancient Egypt, where the fertile land was renewed yearly by the annual flooding of the Nile, the production of abundant food crops was usually a dependable resource (Fig. 38). With the assurance that fields would be refreshed with new silt and that water was plentiful, the people of Egypt were confident that they were provided for by the gods. Egypt remained basically an agricultural land with a society that was based on the tilling of the soil, and agriculture in one form or another was the main occupation of the greater part of the population.

Food was plentiful except in times when the annual flood was irregular, either too low or too high. To counter periods of inadequate production or natural threats to the supply, the Egyptians developed methods of food storage and preservation early in their history. The plagues described in the Bible certainly give some indications of the natural phenomena that had their effects on Egyptian agriculture. These exceptional occurrences could possibly be anticipated and provided for by stockpiling foodstuffs. It is probable that all levels of the population had enough to eat, although times of famine were also recorded. The primary difference was that the higher classes had larger resources to choose from and consequently a more varied diet.

As it is with many aspects of living in ancient Egypt discussed in this book, the evidence for the production, processing, and utilization of a useful range of food crops comes from several different sources. Some of the most important keys to studying the methods of Egyptian agriculture are the numerous tomb reliefs and examples of painting that illustrate the activities of the field and the estate. These

FIGURE 38   A pile of food offerings. Dynasty Five or Six
Tomb unknown, probably at Saqqara
This fragment from a tomb wall illustrates some of the foodstuffs available to the
ancient Egyptians. These include ducks and geese, cucumbers (or squash), let-
tuce, figs, a side of ribs at the top, and parts of other cuts of meat.
Collection of the Detroit Institute of Arts.

are supplemented by written documentation in the form of lists, letters, and bills or memos of sale that discuss simple matters such as the amounts of produce of a farm or an estate, the times of sowing and reaping, and even the allocations of rations to work gangs. Some of the ancient Greek and Roman authors also give details about diet and agriculture when they describe the customs of the Egyptians, but these must be considered for the time in which they were written and how their accounts might have been colored by their own cultural biases.

Archaeological excavation has produced examples of the tools and the containers used in farm activities. Actual samples of food, such as loaves of bread, preserved cuts of meat, and dressed fowl, have been found in tombs. Archaeobotanical study, through the scientific examination of seeds, husks, and other plant residue, has also increased our knowledge of the range of foods available. Finally, the observation of contemporary farm activities in modern circumstances that are thought to compare with those in ancient times may lead to further speculation and insight into ancient practices. In many instances the farming techniques of the modern Egyptians can be observed with the possibility of gaining some idea of how their ancestors may have worked.

It is difficult to generalize about the diet – the food and drink – of all of the ancient Egyptians. The artistic representations and lists of offerings for the dead in the tombs, as well as remains of food and models of food meant for the spirit, all can be assumed to apply to the affluent, well-to-do nobility. What the ordinary workers consumed on a day-to-day basis is only gradually becoming better known. As a good example of how perceptions have changed, earlier excavators were not aware of techniques that would reveal the smallest remains of food materials such as seeds and husks. One important procedure now used by archaeologists is an analysis system called flotation. Samples of soil from an archaeological site are processed in water so that lighter materials such as carbonized seeds float to the surface, where they can be extracted and studied by paleobotanists. From this technique a considerable body of evidence is revealed about crops that were grown and food that was consumed and even yearly agricultural cycles and variations in crop production. The microscopic examination and further analysis of minute quantities of the residue in containers for food and drink have also contributed to knowledge of the materials and methods of their preparation.

The observation of the diet of the contemporary rural peoples of Egypt and in the Sudan, to the south, might give some clues to ancient practices, assuming that farm dwellers on the Nile today would have a comparable diet to that of the ancient people. The modern diet, observed from contemporary contacts with field workers and village dwellers, consists of a high proportion of bread, vegetables, rice and beans, a little poultry and fish, and very little meat, which is usually reserved for special occasions. Except for the rice, a food that was not available in antiquity, this is probably very similar to the ancient diet of people in similar occupations and positions in Egyptian society and perhaps in other ancient societies as well. In addition to rice, processed sugar, derived either from sugarcane or beets, was not known. The sources of sugar in antiquity were largely limited to honey and some fruits, such as dates.

BREAD AND BEER

Shape these well, use the right amount.

Write down what I'm saying, I have made six portions of *pezen* bread.

Watch out that you work correctly, the *retab* bread should be in good condition.

Bring out another *beta* bread.

(Captions to scenes of breadmaking, Strudwick, *Texts from the Pyramid Age,* p. 402)

We know that bread and beer were considered the basic constituents of the ancient diet and that the cultivation of emmer wheat and barley began early in Egyptian history. Virtually every offering prayer for the dead asks for "bread and beer and all things good and pure" for the spirit of the deceased. But this also represented the general notion that the departed needed food and drink for sustenance. It is obvious that the resources for food and drink in ancient Egypt were much wider than just these basics; the possible foodstuffs available included meat, fish and poultry, various grain crops, as well as a wide range of vegetables and fruit.

The grain crops of barley and emmer wheat were among the most important food sources from the earliest times. Not only did they provide the basis of the diet in the form of bread, but allotments of grain often served as the wages for workmen and artisans. Grain was a measure of wealth — and a base for taxation. Evidence for the growing of grain can be found as early as the sixth millennium — between 6000 and 5000 BCE. As the early dwellers on the banks of the Nile began to move from the life of nomads, they learned to cultivate and process grain, and almost as important, they

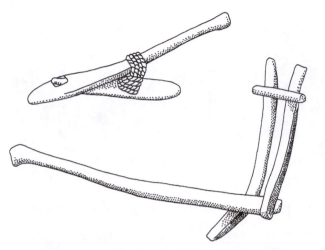

FIGURE 39 Typical wooden agricultural implements – a hoe and a plow made completely of wood, without the advantage of metal blades.
Drawing by Duane Stapp

FIGURE 40 Plowing and distributing seed. Dynasty Nineteen
Theban Tomb 1, tomb of Sennedjem
The couple represented would have carried out these tasks only in the "Fields of the Blessed," in the afterlife, and not during their lifetime. Their dress as shown is inappropriate but the depictions of plow, whip, and seed basket are rendered accurately.
Author's photograph

learned to store it and protect it from spoilage. By trial and error over centuries efficient methods of cultivation and processing were developed. When we buy a loaf of bread at the market or bakery we hardly take into account all of the steps that went into the end product. Starting at the very beginning, the ground had to be tilled, the

FIGURE 41   Reaping and gathering of wheat. Dynasty Nineteen
Theban Tomb 1, tomb of Sennedjem
As in the previous figure the persons represented would not have performed
these duties in life, but the representations of reaping with a sickle and gathering into a basket are descriptive of the process. Even the technique of cutting the
grain high on the stalk was standard.
Author's photograph

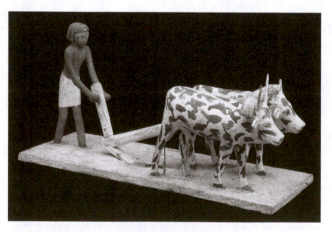

FIGURE 42   Tomb model of a plowman. Middle Kingdom
The simple plow and the yoke are clearly shown. Such models were included in
Middle Kingdom tombs to provide the spirit with the necessities for the next life.
Photograph © The Trustees of the British Museum

method usually known as plowing (Figs. 39, 40). Once the ground
was turned it had to be harrowed, or broken up into a finer condition.
Sowing was apparently done by hand in ancient Egypt, and this was
followed by plowing the seed under or trampling it into the earth.

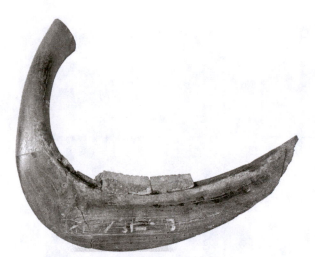

FIGURE 43   A sickle used for harvesting grain. Dynasty Eighteen
Only some of the flint blades that originally made up the cutting
edge remain. The entire inner curve would have been lined with
sharp flint.
Photograph © The Trustees of the British Museum

The fields had to be weeded as the crops grew. After the grain was
mature it was harvested (Fig. 41). This was traditionally done by cutting it high, near the head, and preserving the stalks for animal fodder
or household fuel. The grain was then taken in baskets to a place set
aside for threshing, the process in which it was trampled, usually by animals, to separate the edible parts from the chaff. It was then winnowed,
literally thrown up in the air so the chaff would be blown away. The
grain was sieved to remove foreign materials, and it was stored until
use. The last step in the process was the grinding of the grain to make
flour, which for most of Egyptian history was accomplished by hand on
a stone quern, or grinding surface, with another stone.

All of these steps can be documented either by representations
on tomb walls, in tomb models, or with examples of the actual tools
used (Figs. 40, 41, 42, 43, 44). As an example, ancient plows and
models of plows have been preserved. They are very similar to modern examples, with one major difference. The Egyptian plow shears
did not have a metal cutting edge that would have proved more
efficient and would have made the job a little less labor intensive
(Fig. 42). The principal tool for the harvest was a curved sickle made
of wood (Fig. 43). The long-handled scythe had not been invented,
so the use of the sickle as the main tool required the harvester to
constantly bend over (Fig. 44). The preserved sickles show an ingenious use of small embedded flint blades to give the wooden tool
a sharp cutting edge. The grain was collected and transported to

FIGURE 44   **Harvesting grain. Dynasty Six**
Tomb of Mereruka, Saqqara
Two workmen use curved sickles to harvest grain. They are accompanied by a
man playing the flute. This presumably helped to keep up the pace or perhaps to
make the work less tedious.
Author's photograph

the threshing floor, where it was prepared for the next process (Fig. 45). Winnowing was accomplished with specially shaped wooden paddles used to toss the grain, and sieves made of basketwork were used to aid the removal of extraneous material (Fig. 46). Examples of both paddles and sieves have been found. The grain was then stored in a granary, ready for eventual distribution (Fig. 47). The pervasive dry climate of Egypt and the protection of tombs have preserved the evidence of the actual agricultural tools in a manner not duplicated in any other ancient culture.

The staples of the diet, bread and beer, are often depicted as being produced at the same time or in the same space. This is only natural because they were both derived from the same raw material – grain. Ancient beer was different from the refined products familiar today. It was thicker almost to the point of being gruel. It had a higher protein and vitamin content, possibly furnished a good deal of the daily nutritional needs, and was perhaps safer to drink than water. Brewers' vats

FIGURE 45   Packing wheat into a carrying basket. Dynast Eighteen
                 Theban Tomb 52, tomb of Nakht
                 After the reaping has been done the grain is gathered into large
                 baskets. The unusual representation of the workman who throws
                 his weight on the carrying pole adds liveliness to the activity.
                 Author's photograph

FIGURE 46   Winnowing the wheat. Dynasty Eighteen
                 Theban Tomb 52, tomb of Nakht
                 A group of workmen equipped with specially designed paddles
                 throw the threshed wheat into the air to separate the grain from
                 the chaff. They wear special head coverings presumably to keep the
                 dust from their hair.
                 Author's photograph

FIGURE 47   Model of a granary. Dynasty Eleven
Theban Tomb 280, tomb of Meketre
At the top of the image the workmen are dumping the harvested grain from their
baskets into the bins of the granary. In the section below scribes with their writing
boards keep the accounts of grain delivery.
The Metropolitan Museum of Art, Rogers Fund and Edward S. Harkness Gift, 1920
(20.3.11). Reproduction of any kind is prohibited without express written permission in advance from the Metropolitan Museum of Art.

have been found dating to as early as the Predynastic Period, and other
structures once identified as grain storage facilities may also have been
vats as well. It was long thought that the making of beer included the
use of partly baked and crumbled bread soaked in water as the starting
point for the process. This was based in part on observations of beer
(*bouza*) preparation in the modern Sudan. The natural yeast found in
the bread material could serve as an agent for the fermentation, and it
seemed logical that this was the method used by the ancient Egyptians.
Some current study based on microscopic examination of beer residue
has attempted to reevaluate this theory and does not include the bread
as a part of the brewing process. Beer obviously played an important
part in nutrition however it was made.

Actual examples of bread have been found as food offerings preserved in a number of tombs, reinforcing the idea that it was an
important enough staple of the diet that it had to be included in the
provisions for the spirit. The bread loaves are of a number of different shapes – flat, round, triangular, and conical. The discovery

of thick-walled clay bread molds shows that baking could be done using that kind of device. Bread could even be modeled in the images of gods, as a crude example preserved in the University Museum, University of Pennsylvania, attests.

Much of the production of bread making is documented in artistic representation, particularly in the servant figures of the Old Kingdom and the detailed tomb models of the Middle Kingdom. The stone servant figures include women who are grinding grain on saddle querns and men who strain beer through sieves into storage jars. The activities of sifting, grinding, mixing, and baking are shown in the tomb models with considerable attention to detail. In addition to these representations a number of actual baking sites have been found by archaeologists. One of the most recent discoveries was the large-scale remains of a bakery establishment at Giza that must have served to supply the workmen who labored on the construction of the pyramids.

WINE

There is evidence for wine as a beverage from as early in Egyptian history as the Early Dynastic Period, but most of the detailed documentation that is available to us comes from the tombs of the New Kingdom. Although there are many representations of grape cultivation on tomb walls, wine seems to have been reserved for the elite, whereas beer was consumed by the entire population. The tombs of the nobility often depict grape arbors heavy with the ripe fruit, the harvesting of the crops, and the crushing and squeezing of the final product, all processes that are shown in great detail in the representations. Of particular interest are the illustrations of workmen treading the grapes in a large tub or vat, holding on to ropes suspended from a trellis above them to prevent their slipping and falling into the mix. The last activity in pressing the grapes involved enclosing the residue in a cloth bag with two rods attached. The rods were then turned to contract the bag and squeeze the last drops of juice from the fruit. This stage is shown in detail on tomb walls as early as the Old Kingdom (Fig. 48). The juice was "bottled" in ceramic jars, which were closed with lumps of clay that often had a vent hole to release some of the gas created during fermentation. The jars could be labeled with the type of wine, the sweetness, the year date, and sometimes the name of the field of origin, not unlike modern wine bottle labels that give the information of origin and vintage. The tomb of Tutankhamun

FIGURE 48   Squeezing the grapes. Dynasty Six
Tomb of Mereruka, Saqqara
In the wine-making process the last drops of grape juice are squeezed from a sack
suspended between two poles. After the juice is collected in the container below
it will be bottled in jars and marked as to source and vintage year.
Author's photograph

contained a number of wine jars specifically labeled this way. From
the documentation provide by labels such as these it can be seen that
some of the important areas for viticulture were in the Nile delta and
in the desert oases, not so much along the banks of the river.

FRUIT, VEGETABLES, AND PULSES

In addition to the grains grown for bread and beer, the ancient
Egyptians had a remarkably varied range of farm produce available to them. The fruits included two types of dates, two types
of figs, pomegranates, perseas, carobs, christ's-thorns, grapes, and
olives. The vegetables included onions, leeks, garlic, lettuce, and
celery, several types of melon, cucumbers, possibly radishes, and
chufas (tigernuts). The pulses (beans) were lentils, peas, chickpeas,
and fava beans.

Dates were the product of the date palm and the dom palm, two different varieties; the figs were from the true fig and the sycamore fig trees. Pomegranate was one of the oldest cultivated fruits, and in addition to the use of the juice and seeds, even the skin was crushed to produce a dye. Perhaps not so familiar today are the persea, carob, christ's-thorn, and chufa. The persea produced a fruit that is said to be similar in taste to an apple. There is some confusion about the designation of the Egyptian "persea." The tree from Egypt is not of the modern botanical family designated *Persea*, of which the avocado is a member, so some popular identification of avocado fruit as being from an Egyptian source is in error. The carob tree produced seedpods that were used as human and animal food. The seeds could be ground and used as a sweetener, since they were high in sugar content. Christ's-thorn is a bush or tree with sharp spines, hence the name. It produced a sweet red-brown fruit. The chufa or tiger-nut was a plant that produced a tuber (like a potato) that could be ground, roasted, or baked. It was sometimes added to beer and could have been added to bread dough as well.

Onions, leeks, garlic, lettuce, celery, melon, and (possibly) radishes need little explanation except that the lettuce was of a long-stalked variety like romaine, rather than the head or ball shape more familiar to many today. There is some disagreement about the identification of cucumber, and it is suggested that what is often illustrated in tomb paintings is a variety of melon. The pulses, lentils, peas, chickpeas, and fava beans were among the mainstays of the diet. To various degrees they provided a good amount of the protein in a daily fare that was not rich in red meat. In Egypt today *foul medames* serves much the same purpose. This popular spiced mixture of brown beans is a national Egyptian dish and an important part of the diet.

Common items that are familiar to us in our own time but were missing in the ancient diet include rice, potatoes, sugarcane, and some exotics such as tomatoes. These were unknown to the ancient Egyptians and had to be introduced from foreign contexts. Even so, the daily fare of the ordinary people would come close to meeting the requirements of a healthy diet based on a variety of fresh vegetables, supplemented by bread, and including fish and fowl but little or no red meat.

MEAT

There are numerous illustrations of the rearing of animals for food, the butchering of cattle, and the preparation of cuts of meat, but

FIGURE 49   Slaughtering a bull. Dynasty Six
Tomb of Meryruka, Saqqara
Slaughtering required teamwork on the part of several workmen, some to hold
and immobilize the animal and others to do the actual rendering. One man braces
his foot on the animal's horn to prevent injury from a sudden movement.
Author's photograph

these occur in the tombs of high-placed functionaries, and meat was
not a steady part of the diet for everyone (Fig. 49). The raising of
cattle, goats, sheep, and pigs eventually became an important part of
the agricultural life of ancient Egypt. In the beginnings of Egyptian
culture, meat was mainly obtained through hunting and trapping.
The abundant varieties of wildlife available in the grasslands and the
foothills adjacent to the Nile made this possible. The gradual process
of domestication concentrated on the animals mentioned, as well as
poultry, consisting mainly of ducks and geese. These resources were
supplemented by the development of efficient fishing techniques that
ensured a wide variety of fish. In the Old Kingdom there is pictorial
evidence for the attempt to domesticate hyena and various types of
antelopes, but these do not seem to have proved popular or practical enough for this practice to continue for long. The notion that
pork was not eaten by the Egyptians is a common misunderstanding, derived from accounts of Greek and Roman authors. There is
considerable evidence to the contrary.

FIGURE 50   Catching fish with a dip net. Dynasty Six
Tomb of Meryruka, Saqqara
Two men catch fish with handheld dip nets. The nets are spread
with wood sticks or battens and the results of the catch are dis-
played above, where the fish have been laid out to dry.
Author's photograph

Fishing in the Nile was a major industry. The common methods
employed were hook and line, spearing or harpooning, and the use
of both the dip net and the dragnet. Illustrations of fishing with a
line show multiple hooks on a single line. The hooks were made
of copper (or bronze) and were barbed. Spearing may have been an
early method of fishing to judge from depictions where a harpoon
with a detachable head secured by a cord is used. When spearfishing
is illustrated as an activity of the nobility in the parallel "fishing and
fowling" scenes, it seems to have been more ritualistic than practical.
Of the various kinds of nets, the dip net was handheld, supported
and spread by two wood sticks or battens forming the net into a
triangular shape (Fig. 50). There is a bit more information about the
larger dragnet than the other methods of fishing because it is more
often illustrated in tomb decoration. The dragnet was supported on
the top edge by wood floats and held down on the bottom edge by
stone weights (Fig. 51). The tomb reliefs and paintings suggest that it

FIGURE 51   **Fishing on a large scale. Old Kingdom**
After Lepsius, *Denkmaeler,* Vol. 2, plate 9
This is a typical example of dragnet fishing, where the net is spread by wood floats
at the top and stone weights at the bottom. In representations such as this it is difficult to tell if the participants are standing on the shore; they are more probably
meant to be on a raft.
Drawing by the author

was managed from a raft or platform, but a model from the tomb of
Meketre shows the dragnet hauled between two papyrus boats.

The frequent illustration of the preparation of fish suggests that it
was an important part of the diet. In most depictions of the process
the fish are shown as gutted and laid open, probably to facilitate
the process of drying and preservation. It is obvious that it was not
always possible to consume all of the meat from a freshly slaugh-
tered animal or all of a catch of fish. The preservation of fish, meat,
and poultry from spoilage was a challenge, especially with the limited storage facilities available. The principal means of preservation
before the time of refrigeration and freezing were drying, salting,
smoking, and curing. Drying was accomplished by slicing the material thinly so as not to trap moisture, and by exposing it to sun and/
or air. Drying worked for both meat and fish, which were split and
spread, but it was not used on geese or ducks. Salting, or packing
the foodstuff in salt, either dry or in brine, prevented most forms of
decay. Birds could have been preserved in brine, and fish as well as
roe (fish eggs) were certainly salted. Of the various methods available smoking is probably a more efficient way of preserving meat,
but there is little evidence for this technique having been used in
ancient Egypt. Curing as a means of preservation requires packing
the food material in animal fat, beer, or honey, but there is also little
evidence of these methods having been used.

During the long history of ancient Egypt the diets of all classes
changed very little. The frequent representations of food cultivation,
animal husbandry, and all manners of food processing are represented with similar content from the Old Kingdom to the end of
Pharaonic history. Agriculture was the mainstay of the country and

its civilization, and almost all of the people ate well, although the diet, as has been pointed out, varied depending on wealth and social class. Due to the amount and variety of evidence preserved, the cultivation and preparation of food are aspects of the Egyptian experience that we know perhaps better than any others activities.

Darby, William J., et al. *Food: The Gift of Osiris*. London: Academic Press, 1977.

Geller, Jeremy. "From Prehistory to History: Beer in Egypt" in *The Followers of Horus: Studies dedicated to Michael Allen Hoffman*, edited by Renée Friedman and Barbara Adams. Oxford: Oxbow, 1992. Pp. 19–26.

Hepper, F. Nigel. *Pharaoh's Flowers* ("Food and Drink," chapter 5). Chicago: KWS Publishers, 2009.

Manniche, Lise. *An Ancient Egyptian Herbal* ("In the Kitchen," pp. 38–43). Revised ed. London: British Museum Press, 2006.

Various authors. "Part III: Food Technology" in *Ancient Egyptian Materials and Technology*, edited by Paul T. Nicholson and Ian Shaw. Cambridge: Cambridge University Press, 2000. Pp. 505–672.

Wilson, Hilary. *Egyptian Food and Drink*. Aylesbury: Shire Egyptology, 1988.

7 Hygiene and Medicine

When you became ill with the disease which you contracted I sent for a chief physician and he treated you and you did what he told you to do.

FROM A LETTER

The problems related to personal hygiene in ancient Egypt were not greatly different than in any other ancient or modern developing civilization. It is ironic that the problems were only made more complex and difficult to solve by the side effects of the two important physical realities that made life possible. These were the incessant heat of the sun and the abundant waters of the river Nile. While the constant sunshine was a great benefit, for it provided heat and light and was incidentally a source of vitamin D, it dried or burned the skin and also encouraged the breeding of insects that could transmit disease. The Nile was not only directly responsible for the fertility of the land, as well as providing the most important source of water for drinking and bathing, it also functioned as an all-too-handy waste removal system. The unintentional result of the two "assets" was a continued cycle of disease transmission.

When the prehistoric hunter-gatherers lived a nomadic life and constantly moved from place to place, they regularly abandoned temporary sites that were no longer habitable. In the process they left behind accumulated human and animal waste and garbage that was alive with vermin, parasites, and the consequent disease-breeding potential that they represent. When people began to establish permanent settlements and villages in the Nile valley, this regular process of cleansing by relocation by and large came to an end. Life in settlements brought with it conditions that encouraged the transmission of disease and the proliferation of parasites. For most of the population during the span of Egyptian history permanent housing usually meant conditions of constant crowding, poor ventilation, and little or no sanitary facilities as we know them today.

Water for human consumption came from the Nile or from dependant canals. In the Nile valley there were no natural springs to supplement the river or reservoirs to capture the sparse rainwater.

Every drop of drinking water had to be carried by hand in clay jars or containers made of animal skin from the river or canal bank. As already observed, this was the same water where people bathed, washed clothes, and used for some waste disposal. The dangers of disease transmission are obvious, and the steady current of the Nile was probably the only safeguard against continued epidemics. There are still many areas in rural Egypt where treated piped-in water is a relatively modern novelty. It is still possible to see women and children carrying water in jars and cans from the nearest available source, whether it is a village tap or the Nile bank.

According to late historical sources, including Herodotus in the fifth century BCE, the Egyptians were very much concerned with cleanliness and bathed frequently. They had at their disposal the river for bathing and washing clothes, and in the hot climate they probably took advantage of it often. In some rural areas of Egypt today people bathing in canals and the river are still a frequent sight. Some indoor bathing facilities have been found on ancient sites such as Tel el Amarna, but these were only in houses of the very wealthy and are consequently not typical of the majority of people. In the few such special baths that are preserved, the bather stood on a slab of stone on the floor and water was poured over the head and body.

Soap, normally a combination of fats or oils with the addition of alkalis, was not known to the Egyptians, but natron, a mineral salt consisting of hydrated sodium carbonate or sodium sesquicarbonate, was often used as a cleansing agent. This material was found on the surface of seasonally dry water courses and was easily available in a number of locations in Egypt and the Sudan. The principal source, even today, is in the Wadi Natrun, in the western desert of northern Egypt that is named for the natron it supplies. Because of its desiccating or drying-out characteristics, natron was also an important ingredient in the mummification process.

After bathing, it was essential to avoid the drying and cracking of the skin in the warm climate and the heat of the sun. To prevent this, concoctions were used that were made of plant oils such as castor or linseed, and others were made of animal by-products including fat or tallow. There is also evidence of specially imported nonlocal oils that were probably employed for the same purpose.

Hair care brought with it a problem that still persists today, and that was the presence of head lice. Shaving the head was the obvious solution in a time when there were no effective chemical preparations to discourage the infestation of the troublesome parasites. The prevalent custom of wearing wigs was possibly a part of that solution.

FIGURE 52   **Circumcision scene. Dynasty Six**
Tomb of Ankhmahor, Saqqara
One of two scenes known from ancient Egypt that represent the surgical opera-
tion of circumcision is found in a private tomb.
Author's photograph

There were no other efficient defenses against parasitic infestations
except frequent washing and shaving. Other parasites that have been
found in human remains include the flat worm and the schistoso-
miasis worm. The Egyptians developed folk medicines and preparations thought to be beneficial against such invasions.

Dental hygiene was practically nonexistent. It is question-
able whether anything resembling the brushing of teeth existed.
Examination of many mummies has shown that the Egyptians suffered from a range of dental maladies, especially periodontal disease, but by contrast, proportionally few cavities. The lack of refined
sugar in the diet can probably be credited for this low prevalence of
cavities. Loss of teeth from gum disease and abscesses is frequently
present in preserved bodies, but the most graphic dental problem
often found is the complete grinding down of the molars to flat
surfaces. This was probably caused by the amount of grit in the diet,
either windblown sand that made its way into food or tiny stone bits

FIGURE 53   Circumcision scene. Dynasty Twenty-Five
Temple A, Precinct of the Goddess Mut, Karnak
The second of the circumcision scenes, only partly preserved, is on
the wall of a Theban temple.
Author's photograph

detached from the grinding stone in the process of milling grain into flour. Whatever the cause, many people suffered from such abraded surfaces on their teeth. These in turn exposed the softer inner pulp and hastened decay.

The practice of male circumcision is attested as early as the Old Kingdom, and it was possibly prevalent throughout Egyptian history, although there is not much evidence that points to this. There are at least two available pictorial representations of the operation that have been preserved. One is in the tomb of a man named Ankhmahor (Fig. 52) at the necropolis of Saqqara, dated about 2375 BCE, and the other is in the Temple Precinct of the goddess Mut at Karnak, created almost fifteen hundred years later (Fig. 53). These two depictions span a time period of almost two thousand years and possibly suggest the continuity of the practice. In addition to the graphic illustrations, there are some statues of unclothed males and numerous images on tomb walls that represent laborers and other males who work naked who are clearly circumcised. The purpose of the operation has been questioned and there is no immediate answer. It may have been principally for hygienic reasons, and only later as an aspect of religious ritual. Herodotus says that only the Egyptians practiced male circumcision – and the peoples of other cultures who had learned the practice from them. An inscription of King Piye states that an uncircumcised man was prohibited from entering the temple because he was considered impure.

In the tomb of Ankhmahor the following dialog accompanies the relief depiction of the act:

> *Hold him still; don't let him faint [resist].*
> *I'll do as you wish*
> *Cut well.*
> *I shall do it without pain.*
>
> (Strudwick, Texts from the Pyramid Age, p. 403)

It seems clear that it must have been difficult for the average Egyptian to maintain a level of personal cleanliness, given the conditions under which most people lived. It is also obvious that the diseases transmitted by insects and parasites were his or her constant threat. To attempt to further explain such conditions, it should be acknowledged that one of the most obvious facilitators for the transmission of disease was the general lack of a sanitary method for the disposal of human waste. There has been little evidence found that there was any provision for the regular containment or removal of human excrement, and there are only a few excavated examples of special toilet facilities. At the remains of Tel el Amarna, the short-lived capital established by Akhenaten, indoor toilet arrangements were discovered in some of the houses of high-placed courtiers. These consist of specially designed seats over boxes of sand. The simple fact is that most people throughout Egyptian history relieved themselves out of doors. Even so, there is also little evidence of organized latrine arrangements. These long-used practices naturally led to the continued breeding of flies and other insects and the consequent ready transmission of a large variety of diseases. It also created the possibility of contaminated food from excrement deposited in farming fields.

MEDICINE

The sources we have for our knowledge of Egyptian medicine include:

1. A few artistic representations
2. A relatively small number of papyri that deal with medical treatments

FIGURE 54   Cattle drovers. Dynasty Six
              Tomb of Ptahhotep, Saqqara
              The herdsman on the right has a broken, dislocated, or malformed
              knee that may have been the result of either injury or disease.
              Author's photograph

3. Brief references found in other ancient records, including the
   official titles of individuals
4. The scientific examination of ancient human remains, a branch
   of science called paleopathology.

The evidence derived from the visual sources includes depictions
of conditions on some tomb walls as well as in a very few examples
of sculpture. These include images of blindness, obesity, dwarfism,
broken or dislocated limbs, and possibly complicated situations such
as the effects of poliomyelitis (Fig. 54). Most of these illustrations are
subject to interpretation and some have been the source of scholarly disagreement in the past. As an example, the representation of
a shriveled leg on the unusual stela of a man named Roma has not
been universally accepted as having been caused by polio, and other
causes for the deformity have been suggested. A similar situation
exists with the representations of Pharaoh Akhenaten. There has
been a long record of scholarly debate as to why he was represented

as he was and what possible diseases may have contributed to his unusual appearance.

By contrast, the limited numbers of medical papyri that have been preserved convey a great deal of information on how some diseases and injuries were treated and also give indications of the level of development of medicine in general. The admittedly small number of documents that contain information on medicine and treatment must inform us about the history and development of a complicated profession and its effects, both positive and negative, over the long history of the country. The titles of individuals involved in medicine and other records, such as tomb "biographies," add some details, but perhaps more useful has been the actual investigation of mummified bodies by qualified medical experts.

Therapies that can be deduced from representations and examinations of remains include male circumcision, the use of splints and suturing, and the trepanation procedure. The evidence for circumcision has been found in a number of mummies in addition to the two illustrations of the process already mentioned. Lacking graphic representations, the evidence for the other three types of medical intervention is derived from the investigation of human remains. The process of trepanation, the most dramatic of these, involved cutting an opening in the skull. This was probably thought to release bad or evil materials rather than just the pressure on the brain. Trepanation is probably one of the oldest identifiable operations in the world. Skeletal evidence of prehistoric date exists from areas outside of Egypt, and a few possible examples of the procedure have been identified in Egyptian remains.

In ancient Egypt the medical profession was stratified and specialized very early in history. The most common title, *swnw* (sewnew), has been translated as "physician," and in antiquity eventually it was even applied to the practitioners of mummification. Higher ranks that have been noted included "overseer of physicians," "palace physician," and even "chief palace physician." Among the specialties that can be readily identified are ophthalmology, proctology, internal disease, and dentistry. Most medical professionals that have been identified were male, but there is one record of a woman supervisor of other women physicians.

Actual examples of the instruments of the physician and the surgeon have sometimes been identified. These include cups or bowls for measuring, needles, tweezers, scalpels, and clysters (devices for administering enemas). In the Temple of Kom Ombo, in Upper Egypt, there is a carved wall relief illustrating the general kinds

FIGURE 55   Surgical instruments. Roman Period
Temple of Kom Ombo.
From a wall in the Temple, these representations of instruments
were accompanied by a text dedicated to the god Horus the Healer.
They date to the time of the Romans in Egypt and cannot be taken
as completely typical of those used in earlier times.
Photo courtesy of James P. Allen

of medical instruments available to the physician (Fig. 55). For a
time there was some controversy as to what trade or profession
these images of tools represented, but based on the associated texts,
the general consensus today is that they are related to the medical
profession.

The preserved papyri tell us a great deal about the state of medical knowledge, even though those that have come down to us are
probably only a small fraction of what must have been written on the
subject. One of the earliest documents is called the Kahun Papyrus,
and it dates to about 1859 BCE, almost four thousand years ago.

According to traditional practice of those who study ancient Egypt, various papyri have been named after the place where they were found, as was the Kahun Papyrus, or after a former owner – Edwin Smith, for example – or the museum where they are preserved, such as the Berlin and the Carlsberg Papyrus.

The Kahun Papyrus is a compilation of treatments for human and animal disorders, suggesting that veterinary medicine was not at too far a remove as a specialty from the treatment of humans. The sections dealing with human ailments have to do with female complaints, mainly considered as disorders of the uterus; the animal section deals with treatment of the eyes of dogs, cattle, and birds. This papyrus has the only reference in Egyptian medicine to intentionally bleeding a subject as a treatment, and it is applied to animals to see if they will heal, not as a therapy to be used on humans.

From other papyri it is possible to determine that Egyptian physicians endeavored to treat problems of pediatrics, gynecology, ophthalmology, and the vascular system, as well as venomous bites of snake and scorpion. In addition to the Kahun Papyrus, the two most important of the preserved medical papyri are the Edwin Smith Surgical Papyrus and the Ebers Papyrus. The Edwin Smith Papyrus has been thought to be a New Kingdom copy of an Old Kingdom document. Although it is incomplete in its present state, it outlines the possible treatments for forty-eight cases. These discussions of treatments follow a strict pattern and give the indication that this is really an early example of a textbook devoted to surgery. As such, it outlines a routine based on four phases, each with its introductory statement.

1. "If you examine a man who has … [the following symptoms]."
   [The standard examination begins with an attention to visual and olfactory clues and the taking of the pulse in various places in the body.]
2. "An ailment which I will treat"
   [Given with an outline of the steps to follow.]
3. "An ailment with which I will contend"
   [Given with possible solutions to the problem.]
4. "An ailment not to be treated"
   [Admitting that the physician could not treat the patient did not necessarily mean that it was a hopeless case but rather that it was possible that only rest and observation might provide the cure.]

By contrast to the Edwin Smith Papyrus, the Ebers Papyrus concentrated on matters of internal disease. Significant in the history of medicine, the Ebers Papyrus demonstrates a rudimentary knowledge of the circulatory system, recognizing that liquid moved from the heart throughout the body. The importance of the medical papyri as a group rests in the admittedly limited picture they give us of the state of medical theory and practice in Egypt during its long history. Obviously there must have been many more such records and "text-books," but those that have been accidentally preserved give at least some idea of how advanced medicine was in ancient Egypt.

PHYSICAL EXAMINATION

The process of examination of mummified remains has become far more scientific and accurate in the last few decades. In the past only unwrapping and dissection were the procedures available other than X-ray. Unfortunately, these were destructive methods because they damaged or destroyed the body, but they were used to search for vital clues concerning health and disease in the ancient population. As knowledge has progressed and nondestructive techniques have developed, it is possible to arrive at useful results without destroying the specimens involved. These techniques include computed tomography (CT) scanning, which gives a picture of the interior of mummified remains, and minute sampling, which makes little inroads into the body itself. Such examinations have revealed a variety of parasites – roundworm, guinea worm, tapeworm, as well as flatworms of the genus Schistosoma. The parasitic diseases are assumed to be a major cause of illness, and the Schistosoma fluke is known to damage internal organs and debilitate the person infected. It is still a major problem in Egypt today.

Evidence of other diseases found includes malaria, tuberculosis, smallpox, and rare instances of carcinoma. Among the likely diseases that have not been documented are syphilis, leprosy, and bubonic plague, and instances of cancer seem to have been rare. Unfortunately for the modern scientist studying ancient disease, the process of mummification usually included the removal and separate treatment of most of the internal organs. Without the stomach, intestines, lungs, liver, or brain, evidence of many diseases has not been preserved.

MAGIC IN MEDICINE

The use of religious rites and incantations was thought to be an essential part of the healing process. The god Thoth was the patron of medicine, as an extension of his role as the god associated with learning. Other deities who had roles in healing include Amun, Isis, and Horus. The often-illustrated relief in the Temple of Kom Ombo depicting a variety of possible medical instruments is found in a context that calls on the god Horus as "the good doctor."

Two additional deities also very closely associated with disease and the care of disease were the goddesses Sekhmet and Selqet. Sekhmet, pictured as a human female with the head of a lion, was connected to disease as well as with ideas of war, and individuals named as priests of Sekhmet are mentioned in medical papyri as practitioners who would measure the pulse of the ill person. The combination of observation and derived facts with religious or mythical relationships was typical of almost all of Egyptian medicine. In the medical papyri, side by side with the direction or prescription for a cure were included the religious rites and prayers or incantations to be carried out or said. What can be described as rational or logical therapy was usually accompanied by the religious–magical rites or explanations thought vital to make the treatment effective.

One of the outstanding examples of a medical problem that necessitated "magical" treatment was the process of dealing with snakebite. It seems only logical in a desert country that poisonous serpents would present a prime and ever-present hazard, as they still do in Egypt today. Spells against snakebite rank among the oldest in the history of Egypt. In the Pyramid Texts, which are prayers and spells inscribed in pyramids of Dynasties Five and Six for the protection of the king's spirit, there are many invocations against snakebite. Apparently it was thought essential to call on the aid of the gods for such a serious and often fatal problem. The goddess Selqet was evoked under such special circumstances because she was the prime deity who could be turned to in cases of snake and scorpion bite. In the collection of the Brooklyn Museum there is a papyrus "manual" for a priest of Selqet that lists various snakes by name, description, and strength of venom, as well as listing divine associations with each example.

LIFE EXPECTANCY

It is difficult to generalize about the life expectancy of a population of a country over a span of three thousand years, especially when the size of the population itself is only estimated, but some general observations can be made. Rank and status probably played an important role in longer life, based on diet and occupation. Infant mortality was high, to judge from the proportion of child burials found in cemeteries, as would be found in almost all early cultures. The ideal expressed by the Egyptians themselves, found in a number of documents, was a long life of 110 years. The wish for a long life and health were frequently offered – as in the epithet *ankh, wadja, seneb* – "life, prosperity, and health." Estimates of life expectancy by most scholars suggest a limit around thirty to thirty-five years, although one authority on Egypt during the Roman occupation suggests a lower twenty-five years as an average. There are always exceptions to any general estimate, and the classic and often cited example from Egyptian history is that of the life of Ramesses II, who lived to be more than eighty years old.

Filer, Joyce. *Disease*. Egyptian Bookshelf. Austin: University of Texas Press, 1995.

Halioua, Bruno, and Bernard Ziskind. *Medicine in the Days of the Pharaohs*. Cambridge, MA: Harvard University Press, 2005.

Nunn, John F. *Ancient Egyptian Medicine*. London: British Museum, 1996.

Teeter, Emily, and Janet H. Johnson, eds. *The Life of Meresamun: A Temple Singer in Ancient Egypt*. Chicago: The Oriental Institute of the University of Chicago, 2009.

Containers of Clay and Stone

The potter is under the soil, though as yet among the living. He grubs in the mud more than a pig in order to fire his pots. His clothes are stiff with clay, his girdle is in shreds.

FROM "THE SATIRE OF THE TRADES"

In the present day, consumer society is almost completely dependent on metal cans, bottles of glass and plastic, specially designed cartons, and other packaging means such as Styrofoam or shrink-wrap. Foods that are shipped long distances need to be protected; fragile electronic parts need other kinds of special protection designed for them as well. The use of expert packaging has become so familiar that we tend to forget that there was a time when glass was a rarity, metal was too precious to waste on one-time use, and the whole field of plastics had not been invented and developed. In the modern world, packaging has become a specialized industry where the highly complex design and engineering of materials is intended to contain, protect, and display goods. Any thoughtful visit to a supermarket or a hardware store immediately reveals how much the purchaser is influenced by the wrapper or package.

The ancient Egyptians had a number of solutions to the problems of "packaging." First and most important among these was the use of pottery – vessels or containers made of the local clays of the Nile valley (Fig. 56). Pottery was the most widely used material in almost every aspect of life, and this is well attested by the vast quantities of it, both whole and broken, found on any archaeological site. Although clay was by far the material most commonly used, the abundance and variety of native stone in Egypt made it also possible to fashion durable containers for more special uses. In addition to the two materials of pottery and stone, sacks for dry foodstuffs were made from woven fibers; animal skins and leather were used in a variety of ways as containers for liquids as well as for dry materials.

FIGURE 56   Predynastic pottery jar
This example of early ceramic manufacture illustrates not only the
fine craftsmanship of Predynastic potters but also the beginnings of
painting in ancient Egypt.
Collection of the Detroit Institute of Arts

POTTERY

It is impossible to know when pottery was invented or when the
techniques of pottery making were discovered. The history of fired
clay use is lost in the beginnings of time and in the origins of culture in the Nile valley, as it is elsewhere in world history. After the
development of stone tools, the manufacture of pottery was one of
the earliest improvements in life in Egypt. This made it possible to
produce practical and convenient utensils for cooking and storage of
food, as well as providing containers for easy transport of water for
drinking. In addition to its basic uses for food, drink, and storage,

pottery was sometimes used as a commodity in trade and as payment of wages. When a pot was broken its useful life did not necessarily end. The remains could be utilized in a variety of practical ways. Pottery fragments could be used as a filler material in construction, and more important for history, as a cheap and available surface for writing and drawing. Fragments of pottery (ostraca) were used by students as practice pads on which they could copy texts as a part of their language studies. Similarly, apprentice artists used the material for their sketches, trials, and studies.

The basic definition of pottery, or ceramics, is that it is a material made of common clay that has been hardened in a fire. The ingredients were easily at hand and readily available in Egypt. There were two main types of clay used throughout most of Egyptian history. These are termed "Nile silt" and "marl clay." Nile silt is the material deposited by the river, and it is rich in silica and iron. The resulting fired product is a red-brown color. The so-called marl clays are the product of weather-eroded shale and limestone, producing a ware that is creamy or white in color or sometimes pale olive green when fired at high temperatures. The Nile silt was gathered on the riverbanks; the marl clay was sometimes found on the surface of the ground and sometimes obtained by mining in a more elaborate operation.

The process of manufacture of clay objects was relatively simple during most of Egyptian history. In the first step the clay was mixed with water to a semiliquid consistency that made it possible to remove foreign material such as sticks and stones. After this the water content was reduced by evaporation and the clay mass compacted to a workable state where it would hold its shape as the potter fashioned it. The vessels or objects that were produced were allowed to dry thoroughly before they were fired to harden. The earliest vessels were handmade by the construction techniques of pinching, coiling, or slab, and the work produced by hand building is sometimes so carefully finished that it gives the impression of having been made on a spinning potter's wheel.

Although the potter's wheel does not seem to have made an appearance in Egypt until around Dynasty Five, there is some evidence for the use of a simple turntable at an earlier time. The basic difference is that a turntable is rotated slowly and can only be used for finishing the shape and surface, whereas the true wheel spins at a faster rate and allows the potter to form the clay using centrifugal force and hand pressure (Fig. 57).

The firing process in the beginning was nothing more complicated than an open bonfire. Pots were placed on the ground or in a

FIGURE 57   Pottery making. Dynasty Eighteen
Theban Tomb 93, tomb of Qenamun
The potter, seated on a three-legged stool, manipulates the clay to
fashion a vessel. His helper turns the potter's wheel by hand. The
size of the mass of clay on the wheel is explained in other representations where several pots are shown thrown from one centering
and being cut off one by one.
Author's drawing

pit and the material for the fire piled over them. This may seem like
an inefficient way to fire pottery, but the temperatures reached were
sufficient to do the job. This seemingly primitive method evolved with
the development of proper kilns where the temperature could be more
carefully controlled and regulated. The typical Egyptian kiln was of
a type called an "updraft kiln," a structure like a chimney with an
inside grid or grill separating the fire chamber below from the stacked
pottery above. Archaeologists have found remains of examples of this
type of kiln, and there are also illustrations in some tomb paintings
that show them in use. In modern times the updraft kiln is still used in
some villages, where the fire is usually fed with wood and plant scraps,
sawdust, and dried animal dung. Very sophisticated ceramic wares can
be produced with this relatively simple equipment.

The basic shapes of pottery were dictated by and developed for
their intended use. Cups, bowls, plates, and pots of various sizes can
be identified as designed for drinking, eating, cooking, serving, or
storage (Fig. 58). Typical examples of larger vessels appear to be for
storage or transport (Fig. 59). Thick, crude, shallow shapes were
often braziers or clay pans that were used to hold the charcoal for
cooking. Since clay was abundant and relatively easy to work with,
many types of household objects were made from it, in addition to
its use for vessels and containers. To the long and varied list that

FIGURE 58   Pottery vessels. New Kingdom
Simple and practical, these vessels illustrate a variety and range of typical shapes
used for storage and daily use.
Photograph © The Trustees of the British Museum

includes the basic plates, cups, and bowls, many other forms can be
added. Clay molds for making bread are probably one of the most
important types of accessories, and molds are preserved, whole or in
fragments, by the thousands. Large storage jars were a basic necessity of daily life to hold the water brought from the Nile and for the
storage of dry material such as grain and flour. Some more specialized clay shapes include pitchers, scoops, and flasks. To these can be
added objects that were not containers, such as spindle whorls, loom
weights, and molds for making amulets and other jewelry.

Since much of Egyptian pottery had a pointed rather than a flat
base, ring-shaped jar stands were also made of clay. Clay could also
be fashioned into a ridged platter that functioned as a grill in the fire,
and even pottery "rat catchers" or traps have been found. In addition
to all of these functional uses, offering plates, models of dwellings
called "soul houses," and jars for the internal organs preserved in
the mummification process have been found made of the ubiquitous
material, common clay.

In the Predynastic Period the earliest form of decoration on pottery was a blackening of the rim and the upper part of the body.

FIGURE 59   Workmen carrying objects and vessels. Dynasty Eighteen
Theban Tomb 100, tomb of Rekhmire
Large storage jars are shown carried on workmen's shoulders or
suspended between two people due to the obvious weight of the
contents.
Author's photograph

From the quantity of "black top" pottery preserved, this does not seem
to be only an accident of firing, because its use persisted and seems to
have been a desirable outcome of the firing process rather than an accident to be avoided. With the intentional blacking of the top, the technique of burnishing the body of the vessel also developed. Burnishing,
or hard polishing, is accomplished by rubbing the unfired, partly dry,
"leather hard" clay with a flat stone, a piece of wood, or a scrap of
hide wrapped around a hard object. Burnishing produced not only a
smooth, almost lustrous surface, but it also made the vessel more water-
tight and capable of containing liquids. However, most of the rough
wares produced in ancient Egypt were porous and allowed liquids to
leak through. This was not always a detriment because the "sweating"
of a large water container serves to cool the contents by evaporation.

In the later Predynastic Period there was a great deal of attention paid to pottery decoration, so much so that the embellishment
of clay vessels can be considered the beginnings of the art of drawing and painting in Egypt. Geometric patterns were quickly joined
with rudimentary depictions of animals, birds, and humans. In the
Naqqada II (late Predynastic) Period a particular type of decoration that included suggestions of landscape and images of Nile boats
became very popular (Fig. 56). The "boat pots" appear to record
something of the local scene and the river activity seemingly wit-
nessed by the craftsman. Triangular shapes represent the hills and
mountains that bordered the Nile and zigzag lines the water; images

of long-legged water birds and horned animals reflect the abundant wildlife. The central image, however, is usually of a gracefully curved boat with one or two cabins and many oars. In addition to the cabins, the deck usually has a pole with a standard and a leafed branch at the prow like an ensign. Sometimes the boat is populated by human figures, clearly differentiated as male and female, which has given many scholars an opportunity for speculation. What these early drawings of people are meant to represent is still a mystery, but one theory suggests a "divine marriage" between a ruler or chieftain and a goddess; another suggests that the female figure is a "dispenser" of life. The designs on the pottery are subject to various interpretations, sometimes based on comparison with the later use of the same motifs in more developed Egyptian art.

One curious aspect of some types of late Predynastic pottery is a resemblance to vessels made of stone. Overall ovoid shapes, the presence of lug handles, and the sharp modeling of the lip or rim all look to be imitative of work in stone rather than something made of clay. Some spiral decorations on these pots have also been interpreted as replicating the mineral inclusions in speckled stone, meant to heighten the similarity.

Some shapes of the early pottery are thought to be inspired by imports from the Near East, because they take slightly different forms from standard local material and resemble types developed in Mesopotamia. The design of other pottery with piecrust-like "wavy" handles began their history as large bulbous jars and gradually are seen to have shrunk over time to a more cylindrical shape. Tracing this development provides one of the comparative dating tools for material from the Predynastic Period. From the context in which they were found, the rounder pots can be proved to be earlier and the more cylindrical ones later, so graves in which either are found can be placed in a relative sequence, if not attributed to precise dates in history. The cylindrical form lasts into the Early Dynastic Period, after the unification of the country. A popular decoration on some of these shapes of late Predynastic and early Dynastic pottery is a crisscross pattern that resembles the cord netting used to carry them.

Following the sometimes elaborate decoration of late Predynastic pottery it seems curious that pottery created in the following Early Dynastic Period and into the Old Kingdom is almost completely devoid of surface decoration. After the Predynastic painted wares, with representations of plants and animals, mountains and boats, there seems to have been only a little continuation of pottery painting. Instead the potters of the Old Kingdom concentrated on perfecting a limited number of ceramic forms and burnishing the surfaces of the objects. When the potter's turntable was first coming into use, the typical product during the Old Kingdom was a perfectly turned, carefully balanced and trimmed, dark red burnished ware. The potters of the time made up in highly skilful craftsmanship for the absence of surface decoration. Many of the bowls, plates, and jars from the Old Kingdom are exceptional objects exhibiting a high degree of technical ability and refined form.

The absence of elaborate surface decoration on pottery continued into the Middle Kingdom, but there were some exceptions. Some vessels had complex geometric designs incised or scratched into the surface, particularly those made of marl clay, which fires light in color. The decorative effect was more one of texture rather than of shades or tones. This apparent lack of interest in embellishing clay vessels with color was succeeded in the New Kingdom by an enthusiastic renewal of attention to surface decoration.

Pottery in Dynasty Eighteen households, at least for the privileged classes, began to take on a new look, and a wide range of new shapes and decorations were developed. The interest in decoration began with patterns of lines in dark brown and brown tinged with red or purple. These designs rapidly became more elaborate and a great deal of blue pigment was used. Perhaps the most appealing kind of ornamentation during this period is a type that resembles collars of flowers around the necks of vessels, painted in blue with touches of red and black. These became especially popular in the time of Amunhotep III and his son, Akhenaten. In addition to the floral decoration there was a renewed interest in figural motifs including animals, fish, and especially birds.

At this time three-dimensional figures of animals, animal heads, and even human faces were applied to the body of vessels in clay. There are also a number of examples from this period that are modeled in the shape of animals, fish, insects, and human figures. A special container made in the form of nursing women is thought by some to have been used to contain mothers' milk. In general in the New Kingdom, however, there were more and more specialized shapes for specific uses than before.

The fine decorated pottery of the New Kingdom was not continued and was never equaled in later times. The desire for richly embellished wares during that period, as is also exhibited in other artistic expressions, can probably be explained by the high level of wealth and luxury reached in the time of Amunhotep III and Akhenaten. In the time of the following Ramesside kings some of the tradition of surface decoration continued. Where the early New Kingdom decorated pottery had a limited color scheme that emphasized blue with accents of red and black, the designs of the later New Kingdom incorporated a greater range of colors, adding green and yellow to red, black, and white, but they lacked some of the unity of design provided by a limited palette. After the sometimes gaudy decorated wares of Dynasties Nineteen and Twenty, there was again a reversion to mainly undecorated pottery that lasted until the importation of foreign attitudes and ideas, particularly during the time of Greco-Roman influence.

STONE VESSELS

Durable vessels made of stone had a long tradition in Egypt, paralleling the history of containers made of clay. The ready availability of a large variety of types of colored stone made it possible to fashion more permanent, and often more attractive, objects with no apparent regard for the amount of added labor and time of production involved. The making of stone containers began almost with the first stages of civilization in the Nile valley. The fine stone vessels of the Predynastic Period exhibit a high degree of developed craftsmanship, often beyond the level of the other crafts of the same time. The creation of containers of various types and for a variety of uses is probably the single most significant craft that existed before the Early Dynastic Period. The earliest examples from Nagada I are mainly tall vessels with flat bottoms or short pedestal bases and were carved of dark-colored basalt. Gradually a range of other stones were added for the production of vessels, probably because of their hardness and attractive colors. In the later Predynastic Period, porphyry, limestone, serpentine, breccia, diorite, and calcite (Egyptian alabaster) were employed. It is important to a discussion of stone work throughout the history of Egypt to explain that "alabaster" or "Egyptian alabaster" were terms commonly used in the older literature to describe a stone that is technically designated travertine. The same material is also called calcite, the mineral from which it is made, but travertine is the more correct designation.

In the Nagada II and III periods the number of shapes increased to include round-bottomed spherical jars and bowls, flat-bottomed bowls and jars with convex, bulging sides, small pointed flask-like vessels, and even stone box shapes. The jars are often characterized by a sharp lip rim and small handles drilled to accept cords for carrying. The rims and handles were sometimes found decorated with gold foil, an indication of how special such objects must have been. Other types of vessels that seem to have been very popular were those made in the shape of animals, including birds and even frogs. In the Early Dynastic Period tall cylindrical vessels of calcite became very popular as storage jars and have been found by the hundreds in royal and elite burials.

In the Old Kingdom there seemed to be a demand for more luxury items, which may have also have been visible demonstrations of wealth. As a result the production of stone vessels increased and became an even more important industry to satisfy those needs. A number of different shapes developed. The variety of objects produced of stone included bowls, plates, dishes, jars, jugs, cups, beakers, pitchers, ring-shaped jar stands, and even low round tables. As new mineral sources were discovered a wide variety of exotic stones were employed to make beautifully crafted objects, but calcite (Egyptian alabaster) was by far the most popular. Whereas in the Predynastic Period some pottery shapes imitated stone prototypes, in the Old Kingdom there are examples of stone work imitating pottery, especially bowls with carinated (sharply angled) sides. Stone containers were now sometimes inscribed with the names and titles of kings (Fig. 60) and occasionally even with the names of private individuals. A special type of lidded two-part container was designed to contain food offerings for the tomb. These were often shaped to resemble the dressed fowl or the cut of meat they were fashioned to contain.

With the revival of a strong central administration in the Middle Kingdom a few new shapes in stone were introduced. Jars in the shape of a trussed duck or bowls with figures of monkeys in high relief on the sides joined the more ordinary shapes of jars, bowls, and pitchers. Characteristic shapes of the period included dishes or bowls with spouts, cylindrical three-legged vessels, and squat kohl jars with rounded shoulders and flat bases. Kohl was the cosmetic used to line the eyes of men and women, and apparently a jar for kohl was a part of every lady's toiletry outfit. Kohl jars with men's names on them suggest that they were a part of the male equipment as well. In the New Kingdom many of the traditional shapes in stone continued, including the squat kohl jars that seem to have continued to be popular. To these were added a double tube for kohl and even a kohl jar held by a monkey, its figure carved as a kind of handle. An especially elegant footed cup was crafted in the form of a graceful

FIGURE 60   **Early Dynastic alabaster jar. Dynasty One**
The potential of stone for the production of functional objects was also developed
early in Egypt. This jar is decorated with the name of King Hor-aha, of Dynasty
One, in relief.
Collection of the Detroit Institute of Arts

lotus flower, a type that was imitated in other materials, including
blue faience.

The stone workers of the New Kingdom began to elaborate and
sometimes exaggerate the forms they produced with great skill. The
necks of flasks became longer; jars became taller. Handles were inter-
twined and accentuated by being made more elaborate. Some vessels
made for display were translucent to allow the light of a flame to
show through. The complexity of some of these designs was solved
by making jars or vases in two or more pieces that were joined with
an adhesive, probably bitumen. The numerous elaborate examples
from the tomb of Tutankhamun attest to a highly specialized craft
carried out by equally highly trained workmen.

Throughout the history of Egypt the production of various kinds
of vessels and containers developed to meet the needs of the time and
reflected to a certain extent the values and resources of the users.
Clay, the common and most available material, sufficed for most
purposes. For more enduring or impressive works the rich supply

of available stone in a variety of colors and hardness challenged the ingenuity and the patience of craftsmen, delighted the eye, and satisfied the desire for enduring possessions. Clay and stone were at the opposite ends of a range of materials in value, but together they served for almost all of the needs that are supplied by metal, glass, and plastic today. Once certain craft techniques were established – such as the shaping and firing of clay or the drilling, carving, and polishing of stone – they changed only superficially over the whole period of Pharaonic history.

Aston, Barbara G. *Ancient Egyptian Stone Vessels: Materials and Forms.* Heidelberg: Heidelberger Orientverlag, 1994.

Bourriau, Janine. *Umm El-Ga'ab: Pottery from the Nile Valley Before the Arab Conquest.* Cambridge: Cambridge University Press, 1981.

Hope, Colin. *Egyptian Pottery.* Aylesbury: Shire, 1987.

9 Tools and Weapons

I have seen the coppersmith at work at the mouth of his furnace. His fingers are like the claws of a crocodile; he stinks more than fish eggs.

FROM "THE SATIRE OF THE TRADES"

The evidence for different kinds of tools and toolmaking in the Pharaonic Period complements and helps to explain other aspects of the crafts and craftsmanship. In addition to actual preserved examples of tools, there are depictions of tools and their uses represented in great detail in tomb reliefs and paintings. A third source of information is the detailed models of objects, complete workshops, and their products that were placed in the tombs. As a result, it is possible to understand in greater depth how many different ordinary craft activities were carried out.

The scribe has left his pens, pen case, water pot, and the papyrus sheets on which he wrote. The farmer, butcher, carpenter and joiner, sculptor, quarryman and stone mason, metal smelter and jeweler, and even the maker of mud bricks have all left evidence, either as objects or representations of them to illustrate their working methods in great detail. Such a wealth of specific information about working processes has not been preserved anywhere else in the ancient world. This is probably one of the distinct hallmarks of the culture that make a study of various aspects of the ancient technologies in Egypt so revealing and so interesting.

Stone tools and implements such as choppers, scrapers, and borers that were made and used in a variety of tasks during the prehistoric period have come down to us not only from archaeological excavation but also as chance finds. It is still possible to discover early examples of chipped stone tools exposed on the natural terraces above the Valley of the Kings at Luxor, among other sites, providing evidence of some of the earliest settlements and habitations in that area.

During the Predynastic Period in Egypt specialized tools for use in a range of crafts first began to develop. Implements dedicated to a specific task became important to meet the specific needs of a wide range of uses by farmers, builders, and craftsmen, so individual types started to evolve. The earliest objects we can properly identify as tools were made of stone, bone, and tusk, as they were everywhere in the world where cultures began to evolve. It is probable that wood was also used, particularly for handles, although evidence is lacking. In Egypt the first implements were designed for hunting and processing food, but even in the Predynastic Period other uses began to be addressed. As an important example in the history of Egyptian technology, the highly advanced technique of working stone into bowls and dishes required adaptations of existing tools. A special drill was fashioned to carve out the interior of stone vessels. This is termed an eccentric drill, one in which the cutting head was asymmetrical. This was such an important technological advance that an image of this drill became the hieroglyphic sign for "sculptor" or "stone worker."

Predynastic flint or chert tools developed in design and functionality so that some knives made of the material have become outstanding examples of the stone workers' art. The curved "ripple flint" tools of the Late Predynastic Period were not only functionally useful but of excellent design and are aesthetically pleasing. Such stone knives even became symbols of rank or power and were often decorated with ivory or gold handles. The stone tools for cutting, scraping, and piercing that date from the prehistoric epoch were not made obsolete in the historic era by the development and gradual introduction of metals. The great abundance of chert (flint) found in the deserts on the borders of the Nile valley and embedded in the strata of the limestone hills made it economically advantageous to continue the use of stone as a source for blades and points. The techniques of flint "napping" to produce useful and practical tools continued throughout most of the Dynastic Period (Fig. 61).

As an example of the continued use of stone, the slaughter and butchering of cattle is depicted in Old Kingdom tomb representations as being carried out with stone knives well after the use of metal tools made of copper had become available in Egypt. On the tomb walls butchers are often shown working with a broad-bladed stone knife and carrying an object for sharpening attached to their belts or girdles. The sharpening of a stone knife was carried out by a technique called retouching. This was achieved by chipping a new series of facets on the edge of the blade. As strange as it may seem in the light of modern technology and the common availability of metal blades, there are advantages to the use of stone cutting instruments that may not be immediately obvious. The ready accessibility

FIGURE 61   **Workmen shaping flints. Middle Kingdom**
Beni Hassan, Tomb 15, tomb of Bak
This Middle Kingdom tomb painting illustrates the continuity of the use of stone
tools and blades during Egyptian history. The workmen are fashioning tools by a
pressure flake method rather than by percussion.
Drawing by the author

of the raw material found in the desert and hills and the ease with
which the edge could be maintained were evident to a people with
a long tradition of using stone tools.

By contrast, metal had to be mined as ore, smelted, worked,
shaped, hardened, and continuously sharpened. The convenience, as
well as the economic advantages of stone over metal for some purposes, was certainly understandable. As a result chert and some other
stones such as obsidian were commonly used during the Dynastic
Period for knives and scrapers, arrowheads, drill bits, and even the
ritual cutting tools used in circumcision and embalming.

Stone cutting edges were employed during the Dynastic Period
for a particularly important function in agriculture. Small flint blades
were embedded in curved wooden sickles to produce a harvesting
tool with a keen edge (Fig. 43). On close inspection, these cutting
blades show a surface polish or a sheen, proving that they were functional and used in the practical task of cutting grain. Sickle blades are

commonly found in every excavation, long outlasting the wooden tools of which they were a functional part.

The keen edges of well-crafted stone tools can easily be demonstrated to carve and slice meat, and the ancient examples have to be treated with caution to avoid injury. A simple experiment with an ancient flint tool and a cut of meat will demonstrate the functionality of stone as a slicing tool. It is obviously unusual to find stone tools in use in modern times, but today there are high-tech blades made of ceramic and even glass that stand as modern comparisons with the use of flint for cutting.

Long after they were recorded in the representations of butchering in the Old Kingdom, certain other stone tools were used for a variety of other processes. Hammers of stone were used by the quarrymen in the roughing out of blocks and by sculptors in the initial shaping of statues. These hammers were sometimes just held in the hand and sometimes lashed to a handle. They have been found both ways. The finish and final polishing of sculpture was also accomplished with pieces of stone and an abrasive. As another likely example, it is entirely possible that harder stone points were used in the carving of inscriptions in limestone. Egyptian limestone is usually soft when first brought from the quarry, and small flint points would have made ideal tools for cutting hieroglyphic signs.

With the beginning of the development of a copper industry in the late Predynastic Period and the later introduction of bronze, probably in the Middle Kingdom, tools of all kinds took on a new life. Metal blades were produced by casting in an open mold and were hardened and sharpened by hammering. Such blades that could be sharpened and fastened to shaped wooden handles made some kinds of work in practice more efficient. This was especially true for the woodworker, carpenter, joiner, and furniture maker.

TOOLS OF SPECIAL CRAFTS

A few occupations required only a small number of specialized tools, such as the hooks and nets for fishing, shoulder yokes for carrying loads, sleds for transport of heavy materials, and basket-sieves for food and beer preparation, but other more complex crafts developed a range of particular tools, some of which will be considered here (Fig. 62).

Carpenter: The tools of the carpenter included the axe, saw, chisel, adze, and bow drill. The axe consisted of a metal blade fitted

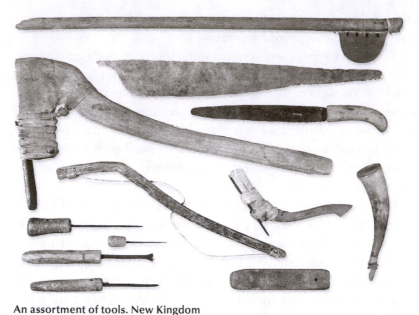

FIGURE 62   An assortment of tools. New Kingdom
From the top: a carpenter's axe, a large and small saw, a large adze, the bow
from a bow drill, a small adze, an oil flask made of horn, four chisels of various sizes, and a wedge. These illustrate most of the tools used for carpentry and
woodworking.
Photograph © The Trustees of the British Museum

into a wooden handle and secured with leather thong lashing. At first
the blade shape was a simple half-circle, but projections or lugs were
later added to facilitate the lashing to the handle. It is sometimes difficult to determine whether a particular axe was used as a weapon
or as a tool, because there are similar examples shown in both types
of context. Saws were very much like modern examples, but the
saw teeth were not set at alternating angles to facilitate the cutting
process as they are in modern saws. They came in two general sizes.
The larger was a type of pull saw used for preparing planks from
the timber. The smaller version was a handsaw that sometimes had
a shaped wooden handle. Chisels had narrow metal blades, either
pointed or wedge-shaped, and were also set into wooden handles.
They were used principally for cutting mortises in furniture or decorative patterns on the surface of the wood or other material. The
adze was the one tool not usually found in a modern workshop. Its
handle was like an axe or hatchet, but the blade was set at a right
angle to the axis of the handle. The adze was used for trimming and
smoothing timber in the way that the modern carpenter would use
a wood plane.

Perhaps one of the most useful instruments for the carpenter or
woodworker was the bow drill. This device consisted of a short bow

FIGURE 63   Using a bow drill. Dynasty Eighteen
Theban Tomb 100, tomb of Rekhmire
A workman uses a bow drill to make the repeated holes in a chair
frame for the lacing of the seat. When the bow is drawn back and
forth the drill spins. The same principal was used by the ancient
Egyptians in a device for starting fires.
Drawing by the author after figure 26 in *Egypt's Golden Age*

with the string looped one or more times around the shaft of the
drill. By pulling the bow back and forth the drill was turned to produce holes, especially in wooden furniture pieces (Fig. 63). This was
especially practical when a repeated number of uniform holes were
required. In addition to its use in woodwork, the bow drill was also
the main instrument used to start fires by creating friction in a prepared wooden board. A number of these "fire starter" boards, with
holes blackened by the process, have been found in tombs.

All of these tools can be seen in use in tomb decorations and in
the elaborate models found in some tombs of the Middle Kingdom.
The tomb models of the official Meketre include a carpenter shop
with miniature workmen illustrating various activities that range
from the cutting of timber to examples of more specialized and
detailed work of shaping and fitting. A chest was included with a
complete set of extra model tools, which gave even more detailed
information about their design and construction. There are numerous depictions of carpenters and joiners at work making furniture
such as beds, chairs, and stools, and even in the elaborate process of
producing the parts of shrines to enclose the mummy in the tomb.
From these illustrations it can be inferred that the craft was carried
out in a workshop situation, with several people side by side, sometimes engaged in working on the same object. The detailed activities

FIGURE 64   Jewelers at work. Dynasty Six
Tomb of Mereruka, Saqqara
In the center register at the left, precious metal is being weighed; in the center, several metalsmiths work with blow pipes to increase the heat of the charcoal fire. In the lower register, collars and necklaces are being assembled by dwarfs and other workers.
Author's photograph

of splitting planks to produce boards, shaping the component parts of objects, and drilling holes to receive the woven-cord resting surface for beds and chairs are among the depictions preserved. In effect these informative tomb paintings and reliefs form an illustrated text on many of the details of the woodworking craft activities.

Related to the tools of the carpenter are those used by the workers in heavy construction. The importance of tools for the building processes is emphasized by the model tools found in the cornerstone deposits of temples, placed there in the dedication ceremonies. These often include model carpenters' tools as well as baskets for moving earth or sand and sleds for transporting stone.

Jewelry maker: The workers in fine jewelry had a rather specialized set of tools, appropriate to their demanding craft (Fig. 64). An accurate balance scale was used to measure the amounts of precious metals. A blow pipe was needed to intensify the heat of the charcoal fire. This pipe was made from a hollow reed and tipped with a kind of clay nozzle to prevent the pipe from burning when it came in contact with the fire. Metal tongs or large tweezers were used to remove material from the fire and to manipulate the hot objects, and small chisels were needed for the fine work of preparing the matrix of an object for inlay decoration. The bow drill was also used by the jewelry craftsman to pierce beads. Shaped molds of fired clay were used to cast amulets and decorative elements for jewelry. Since the molds could be reused, many duplicates of the same design could be produced. Although much of the work of jewelry making required high levels of skill, doubtlessly the repetitive and tedious tasks such as threading and stringing beads into the typical wide collars were accomplished by assistants and apprentices.

Devices for measuring: The architect, carpenter, and construction worker had three different kinds of devices to ensure accuracy for their varied tasks. The cubit rod, a simple measuring stick divided into standard units of finger and palm widths, served the purpose of a tape measure. There were two kinds of cubits, one that was more or less a standard (45 cm or 18 inches) and a second called the "royal" cubit (52.5 cm or 21 inches), which was a bit longer. The standard version was an average measure from the elbow to the length of the thumb. The royal cubit was measured from the elbow to the extended middle finger. The royal cubit was the usual choice in building construction. Multiples of the cubit could be determined with a precisely knotted cord or rope. One of the stages in laying out the foundations of a temple was termed "stretching the cord." This was the process in which the accurate measurements of the plan were determined.

In addition to a measuring device for determining size, some method of leveling was needed for construction. The spirit level, commonly used today, was unknown. The Egyptians developed two simple levels, one for horizontal and one for vertical measurements (Fig. 65). Both types depended on the plumb bob for a visual indication of leveling. The horizontal level consisted of a right triangle made of wood. While resting on its long side, a plumb line suspended from the right-angle corner should theoretically bisect that side. If the point of the plumb bob fell to either side of a median line, the surface it rested on was clearly not level. For vertical measurement a board was used that had two equal right-angle projections with a cord suspended from the upper one. When the device was placed against a vertical surface the cord was intended to just rest against the lower projection while maintaining a straight line. The concern for correct horizontal and vertical orientation is illustrated by this quote: "Surely

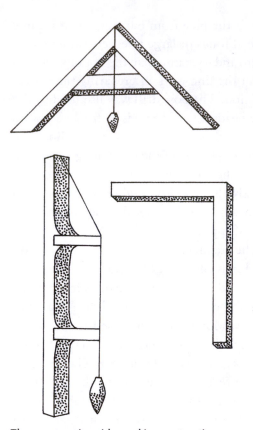

FIGURE 65   **Three measuring aids used in construction**
At the right is the standard set square used for laying out or testing right angles. At the top is a level consisting of an A-frame and plumb bob for testing horizontal surfaces, and on the left is a vertical leveling device also using a plumb bob.
Drawing by Duane Stapp

these things are wrong: a balance which tilts, a plummet which errs" ("The Tale of the Eloquent Peasant" in *The Literature of Ancient Egypt*, ed. William Kelly Simpson, 3rd ed., Yale, 2003, p. 31).

Stone working tools: The tools of the stone mason and the sculptor would probably seem primitive to many people today. For the harder stones such as granite, diorite, and quartzite, the stone worker used a technique of pounding or pecking that employed harder stone balls, usually of dolerite. Where metal tools were employed it was in the form of chisels, either pointed or wedge-shaped. The chisels were fitted with wooden handles and they were used with a large wooden maul or hammer. The pecking method was slow and laborious and certainly time consuming; the hammer-and-chisel technique was only a little less so. Finishing and polishing were accomplished with hard, flat rubbing stones, perhaps with the addition of an abrasive powder such as quartz sand.

The methods of sculptors working in stone can be examined closely because there are a number of unfinished statues left in various stages of completion. Often unfinished statues were abandoned because of hidden flaws in the stone or accidental breakage that made completion impossible. Two unfinished statues of Djoser in the Step Pyramid Precinct offer good examples of the earlier stages in sculpture production. They even include a stud projecting from the top of the head that would have facilitated handling from the quarry but would have been removed in the process of completion.

The process of carving sculpture seems to have progressed in well-defined stages. After the cubic block was chosen in the quarry, the design for the statue was drawn on the front and two sides. The block was reduced, leaving the general shape intended. The master sculptor and his assistants then set to work to further define the image by rounding off the forms. As the image emerged from the block the work was concentrated on refining the details of face, costume, and attributes, probably by the more experienced workmen and the master himself.

Many of the same observations might be made about unfinished architecture. The number of buildings that exist with unfinished parts tell us a great deal about construction. In many cases blocks for walls and columns can be seen in a rough state, waiting to receive final finishing. Blocks were cut to shape and put into place where the last stage of carving would serve to render wall surfaces and column profiles straight and even. In the first court of the Karnak Temple some of the columns that are still in rough shape clearly demonstrate this.

We know from some illustrations on tomb walls that large statues were worked on by teams of men at the same time, not just by single sculptors. This certainly speeded up the process. These representations also give some idea about the workshop methods and routines where the apprentices could learn their trade working side by side with experienced artisans. An illustration in the tomb of Rekhmire even shows in detail the scaffolding erected around a large piece of sculpture to facilitate the action. The work on the piece is being accomplished by a team, where several stages are depicted as being carried out at the same time. On the upper left a scribe is drawing or painting the hieroglyphs on the back pillar of the statue, certainly an early process, whereas on the upper right a sculptor with a polishing stone is adding a finish to the statue's surface.

In strong contrast to the working methods for hard stone, the much softer limestone could be carved rather than pounded. The harder bronze or even soft copper tools could cut limestone. As previously suggested, some of the work on limestone was possibly accomplished with stone (flint or chert) tools. Much the same is true of sandstone, depending on its relative hardness.

Brick making: The production of bricks from Nile mud was a constant and repetitive task demanding little more than some basic manual skill. From the evidence of the remains of houses and walls that have been preserved the sheer number of bricks needed for any construction almost staggers the imagination. The equipment was extremely simple – hoes to mix earth, containers for water to make mud, and baskets to take the mixed mud to the level field where the bricks would be molded and laid out to dry. The single most important tool of the brick maker was the mold. To shape countless bricks of mud the brick maker had only a simple four-sided wooden frame-box. Into this brick-shaped rectangle that had no bottom, the worker packed mud, smoothed the top surface with a wet hand, and removed the form, leaving the shaped brick on the ground and going on to repeat the process for the next brick. The mud was sometimes mixed with grain chaff or straw to give the finished brick more tensile strength. It was then left in the sun for several days to dry and cure. Illustrations of brick making on tomb walls show this process in detail very much as the Egyptians of today still make mud bricks.

Other tools: Farming tools are discussed in the chapter on food, and weaving and spinning tools in the chapter on costumes and textiles. It is obvious that, over the three thousand years of Pharaonic history, tools for the various industries developed to meet the special needs of the life and activities of the people. From nowhere else in the ancient world do we have such detailed information about the crafts, material, and implements used. As a result, it is possible to gain a greater insight into not only the implements used, but also something of the training and the working practices carried out by the artisans and craftsmen as they produced the materials necessary to life in ancient Egypt.

Arnold, Dieter. *Building in Egypt. Pharaonic Stone Masonry*. New York/Oxford: Oxford University Press, 1991.

Brovarski, Edward, Susan K. Doll, and Rita E. Freed. *Egypt's Golden Age: The Art of Living in the New Kingdom 1558–1085 B.C.* Boston: Museum of Fine Arts, 1982.

Davies, W. V. *Catalogue of Egyptian Antiquities in the British Museum VII. Tools and Weapons, I. Axes.* London, 1987.

Ogden, Jack. "Metals" in *Ancient Egyptian Materials and Technology*, edited by Paul T. Nicholson and Ian Shaw. Cambridge: Cambridge University Press, 2000. Pp. 148–176.

Petrie, Sir W. M. Flinders. *Tools and Weapons.* British School of Archaeology 30. London: British School of Archaeology in Egypt, 1917.

Scheel, Bernd. *Egyptian Metalworking and Tools.* Aylesbury: Shire Egyptology, 1989.

10 Basketry, Rope, Matting

As for the grain basket which you made, it is of coarse coiling....
Have another made which is of fine material.

FROM A LETTER

BASKETRY

Examples of basketry have been discovered from the Neolithic Period, including fragments of rush matting and the basket linings of grain storage bins. These prove that the processes of employing plant fibers to produce useful objects date back to the very beginnings of settlement on the banks of the Nile. There is also ample proof to show that baskets continued to be used throughout Egyptian history. The bulk of the evidence comes from the material that has been preserved in the dry atmosphere of tombs as a part of the religious beliefs that the spirit of the deceased should be provided for with material comforts in the next life. There are also numerous depictions of baskets in tomb paintings as they were used in agricultural activity and as containers for the offerings for the spirit of the deceased.

One of the most important uses of basketry and baskets in ancient Egypt was the safe storage of household and personal objects. Since the typical furnishings did not include wooden units that were particularly designed for storage (other than boxes), baskets served an important purpose for almost all classes. Unfortunately the physical conditions of preservation since antiquity were not always ideal. Basketry made from plant parts and fibers cannot withstand the ravages of insects or any exposure to humidity. As a consequence we know less about the use of baskets and other objects made with basketry techniques than objects made of other materials.

The ancient Egyptians were quick to capitalize on commonly available materials and adopt them for functional use. Consequently the variety of different types of objects made with basketry techniques is very large (Fig. 66). Baskets as such were produced in many different sizes and shapes and were designed for a variety of different functions (Fig. 67), but especially for storage purposes. The

FIGURE 66   A covered basket containing dates and figs. Dynasty Eighteen
Baskets were the ideal storage containers not only for foodstuffs
but also for small objects such as jewelry.
Photograph © The Trustees of the British Museum

FIGURE 67   Detail from a tomb painting. Dynasty Eighteen
Theban Tomb 78, tomb of Horemheb
This detail illustrates the use of baskets to carry ducks or geese as
well as their eggs.
Author's photograph

techniques of basketry were also employed to make bags, sieves, nets, brooms, pot stands, boxes, sandals, some items of furniture such as chairs and tables, and even coffins. The importance of baskets to the Egyptians is well-illustrated by the number of examples found in the contents of the tomb of Tutankhamun. In it were more than a hundred baskets containing not only dried fruit and bread but also seeds, spices, nuts, and wheat. In addition the boy king was buried with thirty-two pairs of sandals made of basketwork. It is obvious that the evidence of a king's burial far exceeds what an ordinary person may have owned and used, but it serves to emphasize the important role that basketry played in life and the variety of functions it fulfilled.

The major difference between basketmaking and pottery production is the lack of a need for an advanced technological process, such as the controlled firing of the material in a kiln. In basketry, intensive and time-consuming labor replaced more complicated physical processes. The tools for basketry are also simple and are limited to some sorts of cutting blades to harvest and prepare the plant parts that serve as the basic materials. The ancient Egyptians used the materials that were at hand. These included grass, palm leaves and other parts of the palm tree, reeds, rushes, and sedges (which included papyrus). It was the ingenuity and the skilled handicraft of the workers that transformed these simple materials into objects of daily use.

A number of basketry techniques were developed, the most commonly used being coiling, weaving, and plaiting. Coiling is one of the earliest, attested from the Neolithic Period. In the coiling technique a bundle of grass or palm leaf is made into a continuous coil by twisting and binding the bundle with a cord or strand. The bottom is formed by making a tight spiral and the sides or walls by continuing the spiral vertically. Coiled baskets were made in almost all emerging societies and are still produced by hand in Egypt and the Sudan today. In most cases both the basket and its lid, if there was one, were made from the same material and technique.

Weaving and plaiting are related to each other, and both result in a kind of fabric. Both are the result of interlacing strands with other strands that cross, the difference being that weaving is usually fixed in a loom of some kind and plaiting is not. In plaiting the ends of strands are usually folded back and interwoven into the piece. The technique of weaving with plant materials was used for matting and hangings, while plaiting, also used for those purposes, was also employed in making utilitarian objects like sandals. There were several other ways that plant materials could be manipulated, but coiling, weaving, and plaiting were the principal ones employed for ordinary household use.

It is easy to imagine the woman of the household or her servant returning from the market with a basket filled with vegetables and fruit, bread and (rarely) a bit of meat. What was not prepared and eaten immediately – onions, garlic, nuts and grain, wheat for flour, and the like – would have to be stored and protected. A basket with a cover served that purpose. If beer was to be made, the mash had to be put through a sieve made in a basket-weaving technique. When a round-bottomed jar or pot was set down it had to be supported in some way. A depression scooped out in the ground or the hard-packed earth floor could be used, but circular ring stands of basketry often served that purpose. Plant parts and fibers were bound together to make brushes and brooms, because houses, temples, and even tombs had to be swept. Some boxes were made of plant materials, particularly those for storage of the ornate wigs favored by the Egyptians. In a country where wood of a quality suitable for furniture making was at a premium, a limited number of furniture pieces, such as small tables, stools and stands, were constructed out of reeds artfully lashed together. In modern Egypt there is a class of furniture call *geride* made from the ribs of palm fronds, which attests to the common use of plant materials, but this technique seems not to have existed before the Roman Period.

Plant parts were employed in a multitude of other ways, which included important adjuncts to dress and costume. Wigs were sometimes prepared with plant fiber used as a stiffener or padding. However, the most often preserved example of the use of plant parts in costume is in the production of sandals. The two basic techniques used for sandal making from fibers were plaiting and one similar to coiling. The fragility of sandals made of plant parts probably dictated that they were used sparingly. More durable footwear in ancient Egypt was also made of leather, but probably the more common types were of basketry (Fig. 68).

ROPE

In the modern age we hardly give a thought to the humble material we call rope. If there is any need for it, it comes in coils of assorted lengths and colors from easily accessible sources at a hardware store or a home supplies warehouse. The machinery for the production of

FIGURE 68   Pair of woven palm leaf sandals. New Kingdom
Sandals were made of leather, papyrus, and palm leaf, completely open, or partly closed, as in these examples.
Photograph © The Trustees of the British Museum

rope made of various materials and with special properties for different use has been highly developed in the last century. As with so many of the tools and materials of earlier times, it is hard today to conceive of making rope by hand. Rope is still produced this way in many parts of the world as it was until the Industrial Revolution in the West.

The process of making rope by hand is a tedious and time-consuming one. If it is done without the aid of machinery, it requires patient spinning of fibers into yarn or thread, twisting groups of threads into cords, and twisting groups of cords into what could properly be termed rope. By alternating the direction of the twist from right hand to left hand in each successive operation, the integrity of the material is achieved. The mutual friction of the twisted fibers serves to keep them together under strain. This is basically the way it was done in ancient Egypt. There are a number of depictions of rope making on tomb walls that give us some information on how it was accomplished. The materials were easily accessible. They consisted mainly of grass, papyrus, and eventually of the fibrous leaf sheaths from the date palm. The twisting process was facilitated by a pendulum-like weight, probably made of stone

Rope was an important commodity, and it was used for a range of both simple and complex purposes in Egypt. Halters for animals needed some type of rope, as did many other ordinary day-to-day activities, such as binding up bundles of papyrus stalks. The shaduf, the lever-operated device for lifting water from the Nile or the canal to the levels of the field for irrigation, required rope to hold the pots or skins that contained the liquid. The officials who measured the fields to estimate the amount of tax that should be assessed used rope in the measuring process. Calibrated rope or cord was vital to the geometric calculations needed for the measure of fields or the establishment of boundaries.

One of the basic steps in the foundation of a building was "the stretching of the cord" to establish the layout of the shape and size of the project. Rope was vital to the development of monumental architecture in ancient Egypt in other ways as well. Without rope, pyramids and temples could not have been built and obelisks weighing many tons could not have been erected. Movement of heavy stone and colossal statues could not have been effected without the rope harnessing used in the employment of large numbers of workers. Rope was vital to the shipbuilding industry not only for rigging but also because a major technique of joinery in Egyptian wooden vessels was carried out by lashing the planks of hulls together with rope. The importance of rope in Egyptian activities cannot be overstated.

There have been many archaeological discoveries of ancient rope. Coils of rope considered to be ancient but of uncertain age were found in the covered limestone quarries in the Mokatam Hills, east of modern Cairo. A considerable quantity of rope was discovered in the 1950s when the famous boat of King Khufu was found at the base of his pyramid at Giza. This cordage was partly the lacing material used originally to hold the hull planks together, but some of it was also found having been tied around sections of the dismantled vessel when it was prepared for storage in the pit that had been prepared for it in the limestone plateau. A more recent find of ancient rope was made just a few years ago on the Red Sea coast at a site called the Wadi Gawasis or Mersa Gawasis. There a joint Italian–American expedition discovered evidence for one of the seaports used by the Egyptians for the voyages carried out to the land of Punt, in the south. Excavation has revealed a number of caves with remains of ship timbers and a considerable quantity of rope that would have been part of the equipment of the seagoing vessels. These recent finds date from Egypt's Middle Kingdom and help to establish that the famous expedition of Queen Hatshepsut, in Dynasty Eighteen, was not unique and was part of an accepted tradition.

Cordage includes not only rope, but string and other cords as well. There is ample evidence for the use of these from antiquity. String was regularly used for fishing, both as simple lines and in the fabrication of nets. Fish nets could be either a dip net held open by two sticks in a triangular arrangement or a dragnet with wooden floats at the top and stone weights at the bottom. Among the many other possible uses, string was employed by the artists in tomb painting to make a grid of horizontal and vertical lines on the wall in preparation for the layout of the design. This was accomplished with a process that consisted of dipping the string in red paint, stretching it on the wall, and flicking it to leave a perfectly straight line that could be repeated at measured intervals.

MATTING

Made with techniques closely related to basketry and probably by the same craftsmen, mats were also an important part of living in ancient Egypt. The materials for matting production included grasses, palm leaves, and some other plant fibers. The evidence for the employment of matting begins with its use as the lining of grain storage bins and for protective wrapping around the corpse in some Predynastic burials. Simple burials even in the historic period often involved matting as a substitute for more expensive materials for those who could not afford the luxury of a tomb or even a coffin. However, in domestic situations most matting was used as floor covering, wall hangings, door closures, and awnings or sunshades. The woven sleeping surfaces of beds were also produced with a technique that is termed matting, but this is because these are produced by a flat weave technique.

In addition to the examples of actual material, some of the evidence for matting is derived from imitations or simulations of it in funerary architecture. One of the early examples of this is found in the subterranean chambers below the Step Pyramid and the adjacent South Tomb of King Djoser, of Dynasty Three. In the passages and rooms the walls are decorated with tiles set into recesses in the limestone, clearly imitative of woven material like matting. In coffins of the Middle Kingdom elaborately colored geometric decorations probably reflect the multicolored wall hangings that embellished the domestic architecture of the period. Another example of imitation of matting is found in the depiction of the false door, an important part of ritual tomb architecture. A cylindrical shape carved out of stone at the top of the door opening was meant to represent the rolled-up matting used as a method of closure.

The use of locally available plant material that could be adapted to a wide variety of applications was an ever-present part of Egyptian life. Plant elements were imitated in stone architecture almost from the beginning of Egyptian history. This was a vivid reminder of early construction that had relied on reeds, rushes, papyrus, and palm to provide structural elements. Temporary sunshades and windbreaks made of reeds and stalks were used in antiquity and are still used by field workers in Egypt today. The manipulation of natural resources such as grasses and plant fibers for practical and useful purposes such as basketry, rope, and matting illustrates once again the ingenuity of the ancient peoples in taking advantage of what was plentiful and close at hand.

Teeter, Emily. "Techniques and Terminology of Rope-Making in Ancient Egypt." *The Journal of Egyptian Archaeology* 73 (1987), 71–77.

Wendrich, Willemina Z. "Basketry" in *Ancient Egyptian Material and Technology*, edited by Paul T. Nicholson and Ian Shaw. Cambridge: Cambridge University Press, 2000. Pp. 254–267.

11   Faience and Glass

… the maker of faience for the god Amun, Rekhamun

FROM A PERSONAL STELA

EGYPTIAN FAIENCE

Scholars and excavators once applied the designation "faience" to a class of glazed material found in Egypt because it had a superficial resemblance to the glazed pottery made in the Italian region of Faenza. As is true with a number of early designations for Egyptian materials, objects, and types, faience has become a traditional term even though it is incorrect. It is better to differentiate it from the European pottery by referring to it as "Egyptian faience." It is not ceramic, if the definition of *ceramic* is restricted to material made from clay. The word "ceramic," after all, is derived from the Greek word *keramos*, which means "potter's clay." There is no clay in Egyptian faience except rather late in history, when some objects were made with an admixture of clay to the faience material.

Egyptian faience is a material composed of crushed or powdered quartzite (silica) with the addition of an alkali in the form of plant ash or natron, a naturally occurring soda (sodium sesquicarbonate) found in the deserts of Egypt, particularly in the Wadi Natrun, to the west of the Nile in the north. The ash or soda acts as a flux that makes it possible for the heated silica to fuse and become glassy by reducing the melting point of the silica. In addition to the two main constitutions, silica and alkali, a small amount of lime or other minerals, particularly copper compounds, were added to provide color. In experiments attempting to produce faience in modern times it has been estimated that faience fused at temperatures between 800 and 1,000 degrees centigrade, well within the limits possible with the ancient kilns.

The development of Egyptian faience and the similar material glass are very closely related in the history of technology, but the two are distinct and served different purposes. Today it is usual and expected to have plates, bowls, and cups that are made of a material that is impervious to liquid. These are often composed of a ceramic base with a glazed surface. This was not true in ancient Egypt. One of the curiosities of Egyptian history is that household pottery vessels and bowls were rarely glazed. The known methods of glazing were used for many purposes but not principally for household use. The origins of glazing and the techniques of firing natural materials in an open fire or oven or a kiln to a point where they fuse or melt are lost in the earliest history of civilization. In Egypt there is considerable evidence that the early dwellers on the shores of the Nile somehow became aware that they could combine pulverized quartzite or sand with plant ash, or the natural soda mentioned, that would somehow, even magically, form a glassy material. The evidence from the Predynastic Period is mainly in the form of glazed beads, usually carved from the soft stone steatite.

It was always something of a mystery to scholars as to how Egyptian faience was made until relatively recently. There were several theories attempting to explain the process, but experimentation has indicated that the most common method was one that chemists termed "self-glazing." In this process the soluble salts migrated to the surface of the object after it was formed and partially dried. It was then put into the oven or kiln, and when the surface reached a high enough temperature the salts on the surface melted together and formed a glaze. Broken bits of faience show that the interior core resembles fine sandstone, whereas the surface has the appearance of a thin glassy skin (Fig. 69). Although most examples of Egyptian faience are blue, green, or blue-green, from the addition of copper compounds, there was a much larger range of colors possible, including black, yellow, white, and even lavender, possibilities limited only by the types of minerals added to the mix.

In addition to the technique of self-glazing described previously there were two other methods for glazing objects with Egyptian faience. In the first the object was covered with the glazing powdered material and placed in a container such as a bowl or a crucible. The container and the object were put into the kiln and with heat the powder fused on the surface of the object. In the second method the materials for glazing were mixed with water and applied like paint and then fired. This process often resulted in an uneven surface and variable coloring.

The basic shapes of faience vessels and objects can be fashioned in two distinct ways, by molding and by modeling. Molding requires a prepared negative form or mold into which the body material

FIGURE 69   Fragment of a figurine made of Egyptian faience. Middle Kingdom?
This broken object allows a view of the interior and the sandy nature of the body
material as contrasted with the blue glaze.
Private collection

is pressed. After partial hardening the object is removed from the
mold and sometimes finished by sharpening details by hand with
sharp or pointed instruments before firing. Modeling simply refers
to working the material as if it were clay and shaping it by pinching, pressing, and smoothing until the desired shape is achieved.
Naturally objects made in a mold could be duplicated as often as
wanted, while hand-modeled objects were virtually unique. Molds
were commonly used for amulets and small figurines where large
quantities were needed.

    Among the variety of objects made from Egyptian faience,
the types most often preserved and most familiar today are different kinds of jewelry elements, including beads and amulets. Other
faience objects included small mummiform figures called *shabtis*
and some types of special bowls, drinking vessels, and containers (Fig. 70). Probably the single most important type of object
made from Egyptian faience was the simple bead. Egyptian costume was consistently enhanced by jewelry (see also Chapter 4),
and two of the most common and long-lasting types of decoration
included necklaces and beaded collars. These were composed not
only of tubular-shaped beads of blue or blue-green, but sometimes
with amulets and other elements shaped like flower petals in naturalistic colors. The next most popular object made from Egyptian

FIGURE 70   Lotus cup made of Egyptian faience. Dynasty Eighteen
Faience could be made using molds or hand modeled. Cups such as
this one were probably made in a mold and perhaps of two pieces
that were joined.
Photograph © The Trustees of the British Museum

faience was certainly the amulet (Fig. 71). Amulets were charms to
ward off evils or impart strengths, worn by the living and fastened
to the mummy after death. They were fashioned in the shape of
hieroglyphs, images of gods, and shapes representing or symbolizing
desirable attributes or powers. Although amulets could be made of
various colored stones or even precious metals, by far the majority of
amulets were made from Egyptian faience.

The mummiform *shabti* figure was one of the most recognizable
types of objects to be produced from the material. From the middle
Kingdom on most tombs included a number of these small images
meant to act as substitute workmen to aid the deceased's spirit in the
next life. *Shabtis* could be made from a number of different materials, but the majority of them that have come down to us are bright
blue figures with painted details in black. They vary considerably in
quality depending on what the tomb owner could afford, and they
can also range from miniature masterpieces of sculpture to almost
shapeless blobs.

There has been some discussion in the past that Egyptian faience
must have been considered as a cheap or economical substitute for
more costly materials such as semiprecious stones. It was relatively
easy to produce from commonly found materials and it was used to

FIGURE 71   Eye of Horus amulet made of Egyptian faience. Ptolemaic Period
The many different kinds of amulets used and treasured by the Egyptians were
made of a variety of material, but Egyptian faience was the most popular. This eye
was made in a mold and has a piercing that makes it possible to string it on a wire
or cord.
Private collection

produce simple objects like beads and amulets. On careful consideration it seems to have been considered important in its own right and could be utilized as if it were equally as valuable as lapis lazuli and other colored stones. Objects made of Egyptian faience are often found in the contents of royal tombs and temples, both places where a less expensive replacement might have seemed inappropriate. The Egyptian name for the material – *tjehnet*, "that which is brilliant" – seems to bear this out, and there are various associations of it with the goddess Hathor, who was the patron of the material and the craft and as such was worshipped as the Mistress of Turquoise and the Mistress of Faience.

Egyptian faience was a part of the life of the ordinary Egyptian from the earliest days of the civilization, beginning when people first settled on the banks of the Nile. As a material and an industry it persisted as one of the most typical products of Egyptian culture for more than three thousand years. The average workman or woman might have owned a few strings of tubular beads and a few modest amulets of their favorite gods or as personal protection against ills and bad luck. Those higher in rank would have had more elaborate examples of faience jewelry and better crafted amulets. The truly affluent had the resources to possess bowls and ointment jars, containers, vessels, and miniature images of the gods, all carefully made from the material. It was with royalty and in the decoration of the temples that the highest levels of craftsmen in faience could truly excel. Ritual vessels for the temple and tile decorations for the walls of palaces and temples attest to this.

GLASS

The basic difference between Egyptian faience and glass depends on the effects of a more advanced technology. In order to make glass the raw materials have to be heated at a much higher temperature in excess of 1,000 degrees centigrade to fuse completely. Unlike faience, glass can be manipulated into shapes and forms while it is in a hot, nearly molten, plastic state. Although the materials and techniques of Egyptian faience and glass production are a bit similar, glass as a material has a much more limited history in ancient Egypt. Sporadic examples of what appear to be early specimens of glass beads and scarabs have been found, but their age or historical period is not certain because the context where they were discovered is not always securely dated. It was not until around 1500 BCE that glass began to take a prominent place among the crafts of Egypt. It appeared suddenly, fully developed, during the reign of Thutmosis III, suggesting the possibility that this Pharoah might have brought Mesopotamian glass artists/craftsmen back to Egypt along with other booty from his campaigns. After the sudden introduction of the glass-making techniques, Egyptian artists quickly began to create their own shapes, colors, and decorative styles. The outstanding examples of locally produced glass are from the New Kingdom, beginning in Dynasty Eighteen (Fig. 72). It is somewhat curious that glass was such a late addition to the decorative arts of Egypt, whereas faience had been made and known since the beginnings of Egyptian history.

Most objects of glass from Egypt are small, usually functioning as containers for perfumes, unguents, and kohl, the eyeliner so much favored by men and women alike. These vessels can be extremely beautiful, combining colored glass of blue, white, and yellow in intricate patterns and designs (Fig. 73). It is clear that these objects were luxury items, made in dedicated workshops for royalty and the elite. The technical requirements for the manipulation of the material and the high aesthetic sense displayed demanded training, specialization, and resources that were obviously unavailable to the general population.

In the glass produced in the New Kingdom, a technique called "core-forming" was used to produce hollow vessels (Figs. 72, 73).

FIGURE 72   **A glass flask. Dynasty Eighteen**
This object is a clear demonstration of the sophisticated techniques used in Egypt
for a brief time in the New Kingdom.
Photograph © The Trustees of the British Museum

A core in the desired shape of the vessel's interior was fashioned
of clay, dung, or other plant material, usually over a wood handle.
The core was then either dipped into molten glass or, more likely,
was coated by trailing glass coils around it. An alternate theory
suggests that powdered glass was moistened and patted onto the
core little by little and heated over a controlled flame. Different
colors of glass could be trailed over the covered core to produce
patterns. The still soft colored bands could then be pulled up and
down to enliven the surface with feather or swag designs. Handles
were added separately; bases and sometimes rims were either added
or drawn from the body of the object. The results of this intricate and lengthy process were small, exquisite containers for costly
substances.

In addition to core-forming, glass could also be cast in molds,
like faience. Inlays for furniture, elaborate jewelry, and sculpture,
tiles for wall decoration, and other embellishments were made this
way. Some larger cast objects were fashioned, or at least finished,
by grinding and polishing. The achievements in glass production of
the later New Kingdom were never repeated, but glass continued
to be made in ancient Egypt in a variety of techniques and forms.
However, the methods of manufacture remained too complicated
and glass too costly for it to be in widespread use. The common

FIGURE 73   Kohl tube in the shape of a palm column. Dynasty Eighteen
              Kohl, eye cosmetic, was often kept in containers of elegance and
              beautiful design, such as this one. The developed techniques of
              glassmaking lent themselves to such objects very well.
              Courtesy of the Walters Art Museum

technique of glass blowing was not invented (or did not become widespread) until about 50 BCE. Most ancient Egyptians would probably never have seen or used a piece of glass.

Nicholson, Paul T. *Egyptian Faience and Glass*. Aylesbury: Shire Egyptology, 1993.

Nicholson, Paul T., and Julian Henderson. "Glass" in *Ancient Egyptian Materials and Technology*, edited by Paul T. Nicholson and Ian Shaw. Cambridge: Cambridge University Press, 2000. Pp. 195–224.

Nicholson, Paul T., with Edgar Peltenburg. "Egyptian faience" in *Ancient Egyptian Materials and Technology*, edited by Paul T. Nicholson and Ian Shaw. Cambridge: Cambridge University Press, 2000. Pp. 177–194.

Transportation

Keep an eye on the sail rope, pilot. Hold a good course, as you are the "one of the waters" . . . for this is the canal of the West. Keep your course to port, the perfect way!

CAPTION TO A BOATING SCENE

BOATS AND SHIPS

The ancient Egyptians were blessed with a reliable and accessible means of transportation from the beginning of their civilization. The Nile River that made the region habitable also made easy communication possible and ultimately assisted in the development of a unified country and culture. The use of the Nile for both transport and communication was facilitated by the combination of two factors. The river current flows from the south to the north, and the prevailing wind is from the north to south. This meant that boats, barges, and other rivercraft could travel northward with the current using oars and against the current to the south with the assistance of sails. The Egyptians demonstrated the importance of this simple rule of river navigation even for the spirit in the next life by representations in the tombs illustrating boats with sails both furled and deployed.

The earliest evidence for water transport can be found in a series of crude clay models of a canoe-like craft that are dated to the early Badarian Period (5500–4000 BCE). More complete representations of complicated vessels are shown in designs on later Predynastic pottery (3500–3150 BCE) (Fig. 56). These early drawings and paintings depict boats complete with cabins, with many oars, flagpoles, and standards. Although the oarsmen are not shown, there are sometimes male and female figures standing on the roofs of the cabins. These images have caused a good deal of speculation as to their meaning and symbolism. They may have religious significance, and there are several suggested interpretations, but it is not possible to completely explain them. In any case, the boats depicted seem to be large and need to be propelled by large bodies of oarsmen. Often on the prow and on the cabins there are decorations in the form of tree branches and totem-like emblems. These branches and emblems

FIGURE 74   A large vessel capable of navigation on the Nile or the sea. Dynasty
                 Eighteen
                 Theban Tomb 100, tomb of Rekhmire
                 Although the sail is unfurled, the crew aids the forward motion with
                 what look like punting poles rather than oars.
                 Author's photograph

may have religious or even geographical meanings, but these are also
not completely understood. It is thought that some of the totems
refer to clans, tribes, or regions and home ports, all interesting ideas
but difficult to prove. It is enough to say that we have good evidence that the advantages of river transport were utilized early in the
prehistoric period and that the construction and use of rivercraft is
documented during the formative period of the Egyptian state and
even before the development of writing.

The craft of boatbuilding soon evolved into one of the most
highly developed and important skills in ancient Egypt, involving
scores of trained and expert craftsmen. Further sources of information on river and seagoing craft can be derived from the many later
representations of boats in tombs and on temple walls. These show
many details of design, construction, rigging, and ship handling (Fig.
74). It is remarkable to note that there are also about twenty examples of actual boats of various sizes that have been preserved. These
include craft that were buried as a part of the funeral preparations for
a king and as a consequence are extraordinary because they are often

unusually large. These are supplemented by a great number of models of various kinds of vessels made for the tombs. The models come mainly from the Middle Kingdom, when they were an important part of the preparation for the afterlife of the elite and the nobility.

The remains of a total of fourteen full-sized boats dating to Dynasty One (3100–3050 BCE) were found at Abydos, and they are among the earliest preserved evidence of watercraft from anywhere in the ancient world. A more famous and somewhat later example is a boat found in a specially prepared pit beside the Great Pyramid of Khufu. A second example from the same site that has been known for some time to exist has recently become the subject of a second restoration project. Because such craft were made for the ruler and served in the ritual of the dead king's spirit in the next life, they can hardly be considered typical of Egyptian boats in general, but they do demonstrate the basic aspects of shipbuilding as well as the high level of craftsmanship already developed early in the Old Kingdom and present in Dynasty Four.

The boat of King Khufu is an amazing example of woodworking made from cedar, a dense and durable wood. Cedar is not native to Egypt and had to be imported from the eastern Mediterranean. From prow to stern Khufu's boat measures 43 meters (135 feet), and the shortest plank used in its hull construction is 7 meters (almost 23 feet) long. Even though it is extraordinary in size, studies of this boat reveal many of the typical characteristics of Egyptian wood boatbuilding. The thick planks of the hull were held together by a combination of mortise and tenon joints and rope lashing, and it has been estimated that almost a mile of rope went into the construction. Unlike modern boat construction, the framing or skeleton of the vessel was not the first part to be built. It was a matter of fashioning the shell and then inserting the framework to strengthen the craft. The Greek historian Herodotus, writing in the fifth century BCE, said,

> They cut a quantity of planks about two cubits [about 40 inches] in length, arranging the planks like bricks and attaching them by ties to a number of long stakes or poles till the hull is complete. They give the boat no ribs, but caulk the seams with papyrus from inside. (Herodotus, *Histories*, Book II, p. 96) (Fig. 73)

Apparently Herodotus found the Egyptian system of shipbuilding unusual enough to need explanation and merit comment. If the information derived from the one royal boat at the pyramids was not enough, the second that was discovered at Giza, still in place in its pit, may add even more to our knowledge of shipbuilding.

By contrast to the royal ships with their obvious religious significance, the paintings on private tomb walls and the model boats made for the tombs of nobility give a more complete idea of the approximately 120 different types of crafts that have been recognized and studied. Since the models were made to provide the spirit of the dead with some of the comforts and necessities of life, transportation on the river was obviously important. The flotilla of models found in the tomb of a man named Meketre, a high official of the early Twelfth Dynasty (around 1990–1960 BCE), includes a remarkable range of boat types. These illustrate many different kinds of boats and their uses, both for practical and ritual purposes. They range from papyrus rafts or fishing vessels to well-equipped traveling boats or "yachts," suitable for the well-to-do owner. Even a special cooking boat was supplied to provide the possibility of creating some distance between the pleasure vessels and the heat and smells of the kitchen.

The importance of river transportation cannot be overemphasized, because it provided not only the means for movement from place to place but also the facility for many of the activities that made Egypt a viable culture. There were few roads in the desert, and these were mainly only tracks and trails. There was no other large-scale means for shipment of agricultural produce, particularly grain, from one part of the country to another. There was also no other means for the exchange of goods on a smaller scale between settlements and villages spread out along the Nile. In relatively recent times it was still possible to see huge vessels and barges loaded with high stacks of farm produce and materials such as new pottery under sail on the river and large canals. These have almost all been replaced by heavy truck traffic on a road system that is only beginning to accommodate them.

The ingenuity of Egyptian craftsmen boatbuilders and shipwrights can be well illustrated by some examples of their ability to adapt and meet specific challenges. It is hard to imagine transporting a statue weighing 740 tons or two granite obelisks each weighing 330 tons by any method other than on specially designed river barges. Fortunately in Hatshepsut's temple at Deir el Bahri we have illustrations of obelisks being moved that show how it was done. Egyptian shipbuilders became so adept at construction over hundreds of years of experience that they could face those challenges – in addition to designing practical crafts for everyday use.

By contrast, the boat made of papyrus seems to fit the ideal picture in the modern mind as the rivercraft of the Egyptians. However,

FIGURE 75   Fishermen hauling in their nets. Dynasty Nineteen
Theban Tomb 217, tomb of Ipuy
The details in the painting of the boat show that it was constructed of short planks of wood, as described by Herodotus and as evidenced in actual examples.
Author's photograph

papyrus had only a limited use (and life) for boatbuilding and, from the illustrations available, it seems to have been employed mainly for simple fishing skiffs. Although native woods were not too plentiful, there was enough acacia and tamarisk to provide materials to meet many situations. On the Palermo Stone, an important source for the history of early Egyptian royal dynastic succession, there is mention of ships of cedar and pine, both imported woods. With the limited natural resources available, the Egyptian boatbuilders devised ingenious solutions for the tasks of construction. Using the techniques of peg joining and rope binding mentioned previously, relatively small planks could be fit together for use in some construction (Fig. 75).

Most watercraft of all types were designed with a flat deck with cabins and sunshade areas. All cargo was probably carried on deck. Most boats were meant to be rowed but were also provided with a mast and sail that could be raised on the southward journey and lowered when sailing downstream toward the north. A rudder-like device was provided by one or more steering oars. From an examination of the way steering oars were managed it seems that they were not used as sweeps but rather were twisted in place to alter direction. Well-equipped vessels had a leadsman at the prow who measured the depth with a weighted line. The constantly changing depth of the river bottom and configuration of the sand bars made this an important necessity, bringing to mind Mark Twain's

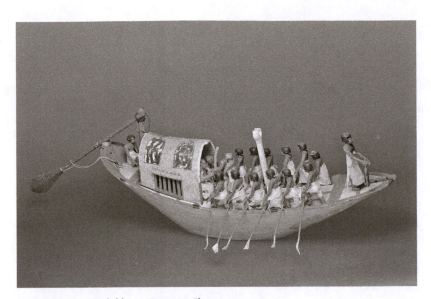

FIGURE 76   Model boat. Dynasty Eleven
Theban Tomb 280, tomb of Meketre
This tomb model is a Nile boat with a cabin. At the stern is a steers-
man; at the prow a crewman measures depth of the water with a
weight. The cabin is decorated with shields of cowhide.
The Metropolitan Museum of Art, Rogers Fund and Edward S.
Harkness Gift, 1920 (20.3.1). Reproduction of any kind is pro-
hibited without express written permission in advance from the
Metropolitan Museum of Art.

descriptions of piloting steamboats on the Mississippi River, where
similar problems existed (Fig. 76).

An important alternate means of transport for goods and produce
was by animal back. Donkeys are in evidence in Egypt from the
beginning of history (Fig. 77).

The donkey had the distinct advantage of not needing the kind of
improved roadway that had yet to be developed, and donkeys were
adaptable to almost any terrain. They were the most popular type of
pack animals and are often represented being loaded with grain and
other farm produce in baskets and saddle bags that were especially
designed for the purpose. Donkeys played another important role in
the processing of the grain. They were used with other animals to
trample and tread the grain in the threshing process. There are only
a few images of people riding on donkey back, contrary to the more
usual practice in Egypt today, and there is at least one tomb decoration depicting an official in a carrying chair atop a donkey. There
is some doubt that the mule was also available to the Egyptians,
and animals that have occasionally been identified on tomb walls
as mules were probably onagers, a type of wild ass. Although it is
a popular idea that the camel was a common means of transport in

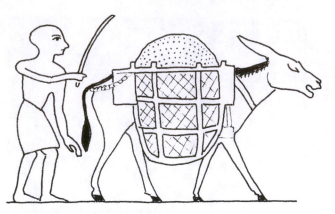

FIGURE 77   Loaded donkey. Dynasty Eighteen
Theban Tomb 16, tomb of Panehsy
A donkey with loaded panniers or baskets is driven by a workman.
Drawing by the author

ancient Egypt, the camel as a riding and pack animal was not introduced into Egypt until the Ptolemaic Period (330–30 BCE) at the
very end of Pharaonic history.

WHEELED VEHICLES

The Egyptian primary need for transportation was satisfied for most
of Pharaonic history by boats and ships. The varieties of watercraft
available were practical and efficient and were never completely
replaced by wheeled vehicles, but they were obviously useful only
on the river and canals of sufficient size and depth. There is no record
of the use of wheeled transport until Dynasty Eighteen (after 1600
BCE), a thousand years after the construction of the boat of Khufu
found at the pyramids.

It is believed from popular literature and most motion pictures
that the two-wheeled chariot was a universally accepted means of
transportation in ancient Egypt. Nothing could be further from the
truth. The chariot was mainly a military vehicle, restricted to the
ruler and the highest ranks of officers. It is also frequently shown
with the king in battle or in the hunt for wild animals, as a demonstration of his fearless strength and power, but it was not something
for ordinary people's transportation.

The chariot probably entered Egypt as an import from western Asia during the disruption of the Second Intermediate Period.
Wheeled vehicles had been known in Mesopotamia as early as the
beginning of the third millennium BCE, around 2700–2500 BCE.

FIGURE 78   Wheelwrights' workshop. Dynasty Eighteen
Theban Tomb 44, tomb of Hepu
Chariots were a useful additions to Nile boats for transportation but
they were mainly employed for military use. In this painting crafts-
men are making the wheels and bodies of the vehicles.
Author's photograph

Illustrations of Sumerian warriors show them riding in what look more like "war carts" than two-wheeled chariots, but the use of the wheel is clearly demonstrated long before it became important to the Egyptians. The end effect of the introduction of the chariot to the valley of the Nile was to make the Egyptian army more mobile and give it a new tactical strength by providing movable, swiftly moving platforms for archers and commanders. While the chariot was not so much a part of the activities of the people, it had an important influence on the conduct of foreign campaigns and ultimately affected the life of all Egyptians.

A few examples of chariots exist, six from the tomb of Tutankhamun alone, so it is possible to examine some of them in detail. The earliest known form of chariot wheel had four spokes, but this was soon superseded by a six-spoke model, as exempli-fied by those in Tutankhamun's tomb. Imported woods of special elasticity or hardness, including elm, maple, plum, birch, and wil-low, were used in the construction, underlining the fact that the vehicles were very special (Fig. 78). The general design included a light body, central pole, and double yoke for harnessing two horses. One remarkable detail in the construction is the lack of any spring arrangement meant to absorb the shock of uneven terrain. This is probably why most representations show two occupants, a driver and an archer. The extra weight of the second occupant would have helped to steady the chariot in battle, as well as freeing the bowman to concentrate on his task of assaulting the enemy.

Most of the average Egyptians had little need of any mode of transportation, except for people engaged in trade or those who were members of military or mining expeditions. The movement of farm products was also an exception that required some animal transport. The typical experience of the land of Egypt for most was limited to a closely restricted range comprised of village and farm. Extended travel of any kind was hardly an important consideration. Donkeys were more useful to workers on the land than boats and chariots were, but wheeled vehicles and sailing vessels had their special uses that were important to society as a whole.

Jenkins, Nancy. *The Boat Beneath the Pyramids*. London: Thames & Hudson, 1980.

Littauer, M. A., and J. H. Crowel. *Chariots and Related Equipment from the Tomb of Tutankhamun*. Oxford: Griffith Institute, 1985.

O'Connor, David. *Abydos: Egypt's First Pharaohs and the Cult of Osiris*. Cairo: American University in Cairo, 2009.

Partridge, Robert. *Transport in Ancient Egypt*. London: Rubicon, 1996.

Vinson, Steve. *Egyptian Boats and Ships*. Princes Risborough: Shire, 1994.

Sport and Games

He was one who knew horses; there was not his like in this numerous army. Not one among them could draw his bow; he could not be approached in running.

FROM THE SPHINX STELA OF AMUNHOTEP II

SPORT

In the world of the ancient Egyptian one of the most human insights available to us is provided by the knowledge we have of the types of leisure activities and competitions they engaged in. The importance of "pastimes" to the Egyptians is amply demonstrated by the extensive and varied evidence preserved that reflects traditions that lasted over most of the history of the ancient culture. Almost all of the activities that can be described as "sport" in ancient Egypt were directly rooted in masculine behavior that had developed out of the early survival activities of defense and the hunt. These included the typical sporting occupations of running, throwing, wrestling, and other kinds of specialized types of combat, as well as the more productive activities of hunting and fishing (Fig. 79).

The foot race must have been originally an informal challenge to prove strength and stamina. The first formal race that we have a record of was not a competition, however. It was a ceremonial race carried out by the king as part of a festival of rejuvenation. Early in Egyptian history it became a custom for the ruler to enact this symbolic race to demonstrate that he was physically sound and still capable of ruling. This was an important part of the *heb sed* festival that took place after the first thirty years of the king's reign. One of the earliest records we have of the *heb sed* is preserved on a small ebony plaque from the Early Dynastic Period. However, in the Step Pyramid complex of King Djoser, of Dynasty Three, there are more complete depictions of the king in relief carvings in the act of running the race. Evidence of the markers of the course is still in place in the courtyard where the ceremony was held.

However, racing on foot seems a simple and natural competitive activity and was probably an important part of Egyptian sport. The

FIGURE 79   **A detail from a scene of hunting in the desert. Dynasty Eighteen**
Theban Tomb 100, tomb of Rekhmire
The wild game pictured includes ostrich, hyena, hare, and several kinds of horned
animals. This painting suggests the hunt as recreation but probably had a protec-
tive intention for the spirit as well.
Author's photograph

first preserved record of a formal race competition is from the time of King Taharka, in Dynasty Twenty-Five, when he is said to have organized a foot race of army units. The course was from the city of Memphis to the Fayum oasis and back, a distance of about 100 kilometers. There was, however, a two-hour rest at the turning point, and the winning unit was awarded the privilege of a meal with the king's guard.

Just as the *heb sed* race was not a competition, no physical activity of kings, such as hunting, archery, or chariot driving, could be considered an actual competition, because the king was incomparable and no ordinary person could be expected to compete with him. The ability to master a span of horses and chariot and the use of the compound bow became royal sporting traditions designed to demonstrate the king's power and skill, but these were not competitive in the ordinary human sense. As it was with all of these activities, the numbers of wild bulls or lions taken by the king were proclaimed to demonstrate his extraordinary abilities.

The sports of ordinary people were perhaps less specialized and probably grew more out of everyday activities. These included hunting (Fig. 79), fishing, target shooting, wrestling, stick fighting, and some types of activity connected with watercraft.

Hunting and fishing as sport, and not as a method of supplying food, were probably still the prerogatives of the upper classes. Representations in tombs show an image of the male deceased, sometimes accompanied by wife and children, harpooning fish and bringing down fowl with a throwing stick. These two methods are clearly "sporting" because the Egyptians had early developed more efficient methods with nets and hooks to carry out both activities. In one New Kingdom tomb painting the inscription beside the images says "seeing pleasant sights and doing enjoyable things in the land of the blessed." That these scenes also had a symbolic meaning concerning the combat against possible evil influences and the agents of chaos does not detract from the idea that they illustrate sporting episodes that were meant to be enjoyed in the next life.

Target shooting with bow and arrow was one sport carried out by king and nonroyals alike. In the case of the king, it was a kind of royal propaganda to demonstrate his powers. With others it was probably part of military training and the constant practice to develop skill. Wrestling and stick fighting were similar physical activities that were also probably related to the military. There are many images of the two sports, but probably the most famous of them are painted on the walls of some Middle Kingdom tombs. The wrestlers are shown in a series of poses demonstrating a large variety of "holds" that seem almost sequential, suggesting the progress of a match, with the two opponents moving from one stance or grappling to another. A sampling of the same types of scenes is carved under the "window of appearances" in Ramesses III's temple at Medinet Habu, where the king probably saw or inspected that kind of athletic game carried out by his military (Fig. 80).

Other than fishing, the only water sport for which there is graphic evidence seems to have been a competition between the crews of boats to knock each other overboard. There are very spirited illustrations of this sport, sometimes called "the battle of the boatmen," in a number of Old Kingdom tombs. The participants use their punting poles to prod and shove their opponents, and the postures and stances they take are among some of the most complex and contorted designs in Egyptian art. Children's games are also shown in some detail on tomb walls in both the Old and Middle Kingdoms (Fig. 81).

Most of the games that are illustrated are the simple types improvised by children that need little or no equipment. A kind of jumping contest seems to have been very popular in which the participant had to leap over a hurdle formed by the outstretched hands and feet

FIGURE 80   **Wrestling before the king. Dynasty Twenty**
Temple of Ramesses III, Medinet Habu
Scenes of wrestling and stick fighting suggest military exercises as much as sport.
They also reflect the conflict between order and chaos, since some of the partici-
pants seem to be foreign.
Author's photograph

of his companions. A type of piggyback juggling was carried out
where the person being carried tossed balls into the air. Tug-of-war
is graphically illustrated with the winning team flat on its backs as
it makes the final heave. Whirling games, leapfrog, contortionist
contests, and games with hoops and sticks all testify to the universal
attractions of such uncomplicated pastimes throughout the ages. One
interesting type of image depicts four youths, male or female, holding hands and probably meant to be seen as in a circle (Fig. 81). They
are involved in some sort of game that might be taken to resemble
ring-around-the-rosy, but since the captions call it "erecting the
wine arbor" or the "basket game," it probably involves leaning back
in a test of strength, forming the shape of a basket. It has been suggested that it was also a spinning game, intended to make the participants dizzy. Another rather specialized game appears to resemble
"prisoners' base," where the captured opponent can be released by
being tagged by someone from his team. From this variety of games
children were probably meant to develop not only physical skills but
also a competitive sense that would benefit them in later life. It is

FIGURE 81   Children's games. Dynasty Six
Tomb of Meryruka, Saqqara
This circle game is sometimes identified in inscriptions as the "basket game." As a test of strength or agility it could be played by either sex.
Author's photograph

interesting to note that most of the games for which there is pictorial evidence require little or no special equipment.

TOYS AND TABLE GAMES

The overseer of the estate, Mereri: . . . a good thing . . . just watch me take it!

The royal noble, Khuenre: You have spoken too soon; the board is mine! (Captions to a game of senet. Strudwick, *Texts from the Pyramid Age*, p. 411)

In the category of toys it is somewhat difficult to determine if artifacts are meant to be playthings or only models of objects useful to the spirit in the next life. As an example, what seems to be a doll may really be a symbolic image of a companion figure for the deceased. The many models of boats, agricultural scenes, and workshops were never the subject of play but were intended to serve the spirit in the afterlife. However, there are many simple objects such as balls and

FIGURE 82   **A selection of children's toys**
These include balls, tops, and a wooden cat with a movable lower jaw.
Photograph © The Trustees of the British Museum

figures of animals, as well as actual dolls, which are most probably to
be considered toys (Fig. 82).

Among the more complex toy figures are some made as images
of cats, lions, and crocodiles that have jointed jaws, probably meant
to suggest their most characteristic or amusing feature. Animal toys
so designed with movable lower jaws were able to simulate snapping
and biting. An exceptional example of a toy with moving parts is
preserved in the collection of the Egyptian Museum in Cairo. It represents a group of three dwarfs standing on a platform designed so
that attached pull-strings caused the three figures to turn, and perhaps whirl, as if they were dancing. There was a range of such toys,
including a jointed figure that depicts a servant grinding grain on a
stone quern, but it is not certain that this example was meant to be a
toy. By far the type most often found is the simple doll. These range
from "paddle dolls" made of wood and crude figures made of clay or
mud to more elaborate examples with decorations of hair, beads, and
shells. Figures of animals, crudely fashioned from clay, also seemed
to have been popular, and clay would have been the most available
source for fashioning playthings in the shape of humans, animals,
and even crude models of boats.

Board games seem to have been widely played in ancient Egypt,
to judge by the number of examples found in the tombs of the nobility. There were basically four types of such games, and the one called
"senet" was probably the most popular, lasting from the Predynastic

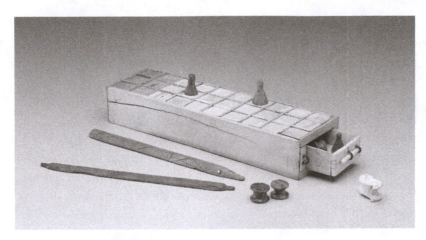

FIGURE 83   A senet game. New Kingdom
The playing surface is on top, and a drawer below provides a place to store the pieces. The moves could be determined by throwing sticks, which were round on one side, flat on the other, or by knuckle bones like the one illustrated. Senit was a very popular game in Egyptian life but also held a special symbolic significance for the passage of the spirit in death. As a consequence senet boards were often included in the tomb furniture.
Photograph © The Trustees of the British Museum

Period to the Roman occupation (Fig. 83). It was a game for two players, using a board of thirty squares. Throwing sticks that had one flat and one rounded side were cast to determine the number of squares in a move. The "passage" of the player's pieces on the board was also a metaphor for the trials of the spirit in the afterlife, so the game is often illustrated on tomb walls. To further illustrate the popularity or the importance of this game, Tutankhamun had at least four boards and sets of playing pieces for senet included in his tomb. The game boards were often elaborate examples of the furniture maker's art, where the board could be designed to sit on its own small table, which in turn rested on a miniature sled. Exotic materials including ivory and ebony were used in the construction of these boards if they were intended for royalty or the elite. By contrast, the senet board of even an official like the architect Kha was made of a simpler wood.

There were other board games including one called "twenty squares," which was similar to senet, and another called "dogs and jackals." Another game called the "serpent" was played on a round board with a spiral track. In addition to the throwing sticks used to determine the number of moves in senit, the Egyptians used the knuckle bones of sheep, both real and imitation. These bones have four sides that are all differently shaped – flat, concave, convex, and irregular – thus giving more possible combinations to make up a move than the throwing sticks, which had only two differently shaped sides. Cubic dice with six sides do not appear until the late New Kingdom in Egypt.

The importance of board games to the Egyptians is well illustrated by the number of examples of the preserved equipment and the frequency of depictions in tombs. It is difficult to determine when they were considered mainly as pastimes and for simple entertainment and when they were meant as more special symbolic representations of the passage of the spirit in the next world. In any case they took the notion of "game" to a much different level that we might at first imagine.

PETS

There is a good deal of evidence to prove that the ancient Egyptians were very fond of pets. Images of pet dogs, cats, monkeys, and even gazelles are found on the walls of tombs. Dogs seem to have been the favorite choice and probably the most important kind of pet, because they offered not only companionship but were useful as watchdogs and engaged in hunting activities. They were given names such as "Brave," "Lively," and "Reliant," attesting to the qualities they possessed or that were expected of them.

That dogs were particularly favored as pets can be attested from the Predynastic Period throughout Egyptian history. It is thought that the Egyptians practiced some type of selective breeding to produce types that can be recognized as greyhounds, salukis, and perhaps basenjis (Fig. 84). When a pet dog died it was sometimes mummified and placed in the owner's tomb, although this was not a widespread practice. When other dogs were embalmed and mummified it was as offerings to one of the deities who were represented with canine attributes, such as the god Anubis.

Dogs are not kept as pets in the Muslim world today, in contrast to the custom of ancient Egypt. Wild dogs doubtlessly roamed the outskirts of villages and settlements in ancient times, as did hyenas and jackals. In Egypt today you can see packs of semiwild dogs that live off of the scraps and garbage near the villages and are tolerated because they serve a guard function. In comments recordered as early as the seventeenth century, travelers often remarked on the presence of hordes of feral dogs that made it impossible to approach a village without attracting considerable attention. It is likely that such situations existed in the rural areas of ancient Egypt as well.

FIGURE 84   **Man with a pet dog**
The elegant dog at his master's feet is called Beha in the inscription.
The servant "bringing the calf" is part of the offerings brought to
the tomb owner.
Courtesy of the Walters Art Museum

Cats do not make their appearance as domestic animals until
Dynasty Eleven, when they apparently became valued as mousers. In
the New Kingdom they are often depicted as pets, particularly under
the chair of the lady of the family. The question about the inclusion
of these images is whether they are actually realistic representations
of pets or types of religious symbols. In the tombs of New Kingdom
nobility, cats are also depicted in hunting scenes, where they attack
or capture birds. In the Third Intermediate Period the domestic
cat became associated with the gentle aspect of the lioness goddess,
Sakhmet, but the most popular images of cats from Egypt belong to
the goddess Bastet of Bubastis. The graceful representations of cats
in bronze sculpture that were dedicated to her have become almost
symbols of ancient Egypt to many people.

Decker, Wolfgang. "Sports" in *The Oxford Encyclopedia of Ancient Egypt*, edited by Donald B. Redford. Oxford: Oxford University Press, 2001. Vol. 2, pp. 1–3.

Sports and Games of Ancient Egypt. New Haven: Yale University Press, 1992.

Kendall, Timothy. "Games," in *The Oxford Encyclopedia of Ancient Egypt*, edited by Donald B. Redford. Oxford: Oxford University Press, 2001. Vol. 2, pp. 1–3.

Touny, Ahmed E. D., and Steffen Wenig. *Sport in Ancient Egypt*. Amsterdam: Grüner, 1969.

Tyldesley, Joyce. *Egyptian Games and Sports*. Aylesbury: Shire Egyptology, 2007.

14   Music and Dance

The noble, Imyhsetj, playing the pipe very well.
Playing the flute for your Ka every day.

CAPTIONS TO TOMB SCENES

MUSIC AND MUSICAL INSTRUMENTS

What is usually defined as music is basically sound and rhythm organized in time, and virtually all cultures and societies have or have had some form of it. In *Music and the Mind* Anthony Store made the observation that in every culture music serves as a device or tool to bring people together in common activities. Repeated rhythms serve to unite participants in recreation and ritual, organize troops on the march, and coordinate the efforts of workers in the fields. Anyone who has ever seen the effects of the "call and response" work songs of field hands, where a leader sings or chants a verse and the workers respond with a chorus, can attest to their rhythmic results.

One of the most serious obstacles to an understanding of ancient Egyptian music is the almost complete absence of any preserved musical notation in the form of written music. There is at least one exception, but one that is not much help. This is a small statue of a harpist depicted with an open manuscript before him. The page has the remains of some symbols on it, probably representing some direction as to how he was to play. Even though it is not very helpful, this object does prove that there may have been a system of written music. However, preserved evidence of musical notation and writings about music theory in Egypt are not well attested until the time of the Greeks.

There are some written references to music and musicians in ancient texts, but nothing that can give a clear idea of how it was organized or even some estimation of how it sounded. Even so, there are what seem to be the lyrics of some songs preserved in papyri and on tomb walls, and there is a body of literature usually classified as poetry that probably includes some pieces that were sung. From the mass of other evidence the importance of music in

FIGURE 85   Two female musicians. Dynasty Eighteen
             Theban Tomb 22, tomb of Wah
             The woman on the left is playing on a pipe; her companion on the
             right plays a lyre.
             Author's photograph

temple life, daily work, and leisure activities is immediately obvious (Fig. 85). The physical remains of instruments discovered by
archaeologists and the numerous depictions of musical "events" in
art are concrete indications of the pervasive presence of music in
the life of Egypt.

The performance and enjoyment of music was certainly as
much a part of religious observances as it was also an integral part
of everyday life. It is known that playing music for the gods was as
important as making food offerings and burning incense to them.
Musicians and instruments are represented on the walls of temples
often enough to make this obvious. Women with the title "chant-
ress" or singer were specially appointed to participate in the ritual in
the temples, both daily and for special festivals. They were called on
to awaken the gods in the morning and to sing them to sleep in the
evening. Chosen from the upper classes, these singers were honored
in Egyptian society and could even be selected from members of the
royal family. As an example, it was said about Queen Nefertiti that
she pacified the god Aton with a sweet voice while she accompanied

FIGURE 86   **Three musicians. Old Kingdom**
A typical musical group in the Old Kingdom consisting of a flute player, one who claps or sings, and another who plays the harp.
Drawing by the author

herself with the sistrum rattle. She is often depicted in temple reliefs in exactly this act of devotion.

Remembering always that Egyptian art was symbolic and not literally realistic, representations in tombs give us some ideas about the composition and makeup of musical groups, particularly those that played at funerary functions. The variety of instruments was limited but usually included a combination of strings, winds, and percussion, somewhat like many musical groups today (Fig. 86).

Harps of various sizes seem to have been particularly popular for different kinds of performances, and every dance was accompanied by some type of percussion, which utilized drums, rattles, or clappers. In contrast, images of soldiers on the march are shown with only drums and trumpets.

Even with all of the evidence we have of the music played by the ancient Egyptians there is still virtually no way to know how it sounded. The most abundant clues are in the form of the real, preserved instruments, augmented by representations of them in art. Even so, the mysteries that still confront us concern the basic vocabulary of music, which includes pitch, intervals, and rhythm. As an example, wind instruments such as the trumpet produce a natural series of tone intervals by blowing at different intensities, but we have no way of knowing how an ancient trumpet was sounded and in what sort of rhythm or order of tones the sounds were produced. Examples of woodwinds are preserved with some of the finger holes intact, which can give further suggestions of an Egyptian musical scale. However, none of the many harps that have survived can offer

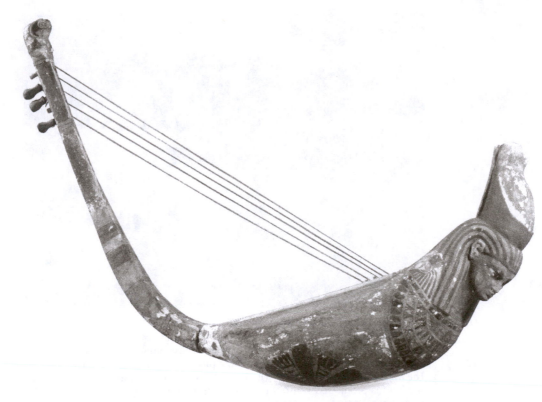

FIGURE 87   Elaborate wooden harp, carved and decorated with paint. New Kingdom
The head on the curved base is probably the goddess Mut, identified by the double crown she wears. At the top of the instrument there is a second, smaller head that is probably an image of the goddess Ma'at.
Photograph © The Trustees of the British Museum

any kind of clue as to how they were tuned (Fig. 87). It is particularly frustrating to students of ancient music that so much evidence exists and yet we can know only how musical performance may have looked and how the instruments were handled, and not how the music sounded.

Nevertheless, the musical instruments in antiquity were not too different from those of today. Before the electronic age there were only three basic ways of producing musical sound. These were by beating on an object or a taut surface (percussion), blowing air into or across a tube (brass and woodwind), and making a cord vibrate (strings). The three basic types of sound producers were used in one form or another in combination by the Egyptians, so it seems that the effects they produced together were thought to be pleasant and were appreciated for their use in combination as well as for their variety (Fig. 88).

FIGURE 88   **Three musicians. Dynasty Eighteen**
Facsimile of a painting from the Theban Tomb 52, tomb of Nakht
This detail from the representation of the funerary banquet in the tomb depicts
three female musicians who play a double pipe, a lute, and a deep harp.
The Metropolitan Museum of Art, Rogers Fund, 1915 (15.5.19d). Reproduction of
any kind is prohibited without express written permission in advance from the
Metropolitan Museum of Art.

The simplest percussive effect was achieved by hand clapping, often illustrated in the tombs of the Old Kingdom. A slightly more elaborate form of percussion was produced by a type of clapper held in the hands. Examples of clappers made of wood or ivory that would have produced a clicking sound have been compared to the effect of Spanish castanets. These clappers are sometimes carved with ends terminating in small hands, suggesting that they were only one step away from actual hand clapping. Drums of a familiar type with a skin or membrane stretched over a form took on a variety of shapes. These included "frame" drums that look like a rectangular tambourine but lacking the metal disks that jingle. These were used by both dancers and singers.

The type of drum employed by the military on the march was a large, deep, nearly cylindrical drum slung on a strap. The other significant percussion instrument was the sistrum, a metal rattle with bangle disks, which was used in religious observances. The rattle of the sistrum was particularly appropriate in the devotions to the goddess Hathor. In addition, the sound of shaking a beaded collar or necklace held in the hand was also used as a subtle percussion instrument in religious rites.

Woodwinds were usually made from a hollow reed and can be roughly compared to the flute, oboe, or clarinet, depending on the various ways the sound could be produced, the type of mouthpiece, and if a vibrating reed was single or double. The instrument that closely approximated the flute was blown across the open end of the tube, much like the modern Arab instrument called the *nye*. The type that can best be compared to the clarinet had a single reed, probably made by partially detaching a part of the reed tube itself. The ancient ancestor of the oboe produced its sound when the air was blown between two reeds, as it is in the modern instrument today. With the different methods of sound production there were also three basic configurations of the woodwinds; the single pipe, the double pipe with the two tubes parallel, and double pipes with the two tubes set at an angle. All of these are pictured in painting and relief carving.

Brass instruments were limited to a type of straight trumpet with a flared bell. The trumpet was a solely military instrument and is often shown as carried by soldiers on the march. Most depictions of the trumpeter show him carrying a wood core-like object to insert into the instrument to prevent bending or denting the thin metal tube. Among the many attempts that have been made to discover the actual sounds of an Egyptian instrument, one historic instance stands out. In 1939 a British military musician performed on one of the two trumpets found in the tomb of Tutankhamun. A recording was made by the British Broadcasting Company, which can be heard on the internet. It can be found at http://www.bbc.co.uk/news/world-middle-east-13092827. The tones and intervals are heard, but any rhythm used by the trumpeter was pure guesswork.

The harp, the lyre, and a lute-like instrument with a long neck and a small body made up the category of stringed instruments. Harps came in two basic shapes; one was curved, with a sound box that was part of a continuous arc (Fig. 87). The second was angular, designed like two sides of a triangle. The arched harp seems to have been a native product and can be seen in tomb representations from the Old Kingdom on; the angular harp was a later import from Mesopotamia, where it was a common shape employed as early as the time of the Sumerians. The appearance of imported musical instruments such as the angular harp and the lyre say much about the Egyptians' ability to assimilate and utilize foreign innovations.

FIGURE 89   **The master entertained with harp music. Dynasty Six**
Tomb of Meryruka, Saqqara
Music was not restricted to performance as a part of ritual but could be provided
on an intimate basis for the enjoyment of an individual.
Author's photograph

Since the native arched harp was an instrument that used six to nine strings and the imported instrument could have more than twenty, the explanation for its adoption may have been that its extended tonal range increased the variety and effectiveness of the performance.

Harps were played by both men and women, but lutes were exclusively women's instruments. The stringed instrument termed a lute by students of ancient Egyptian music looks nothing like the European pear-shaped, multistringed instrument or its ancestor, the Middle Eastern *oud*. Instead, the ancient lute had a small oval-shaped body like a turtle shell or coconut, with long thin neck and few strings (Fig. 88). It is shown mainly in representations of female entertainers at a banquet.

There is some indication that the Egyptians practiced a system of hand signals that might have indicated the pitch. Representations in tombs include images of singers who hold their hands in a variety of positions, as if directing changes of pitch or lengths of tones. This can be compared to a system attributed to Guido d'Arezzo, an Italian medieval music theorist, where each part of the hand was assigned to represent a tone. The teacher or conductor could point to that part of the hand to indicate the tone to be sung.

In tomb representations that depict various activities of the funeral banquet and work in the fields, a number of special songs have been identified. These are known only by the text or lyrics, since no notation of pitches or sound duration exists. From the texts interposed in some scenes it is possible to recognize the work songs, where laborers in the fields sing to lighten their task or to help the time pass. These often speak of the hard toil and the success in labor accomplished. Some specialized work songs relate to the harvest, and others take a form still observed in the fields in Egypt today. These are the "call and response" songs mentioned earlier, where a leader sings the verse and the workers respond with a chorus, often repeated. In modern Egypt these songs can be improvised on the spot and are often commentaries on local events and personalities. It is possible that the same ideas were the basis for work songs in antiquity.

There is often a clear division of music between the sexes, not only in the types of instruments played, but also in the situations in which males and females perform. However, in the same banquet scene female performers are shown near a male harpist but somewhat separated from him. There is also evidence of a professional organization that governed the makeup of musical groups and their employment. Called the *kenner*, this association resembled a guild or even something similar to a union and may have functioned as an employment source to place musicians in particular settings.

One of the most famous examples of a composition, as usual preserved only in textual form, is the "Song of the Harpist." Inscribed in differing versions on some tomb walls and recorded in papyri, its theme is somewhat of the "eat, drink, and be merry" type, but its message is more somber. In part, it says:

Heap up your joys,
Let your heart not sink!
Follow your heart and your happiness,
Do your things on earth as your heart commands!
When there comes to you that day of mourning,
The Weary-hearted [Osiris] hears not their mourning,
Wailing saves no man from the pit!

FIGURE 90   A man, his wife, and his daughter entertained by a harpist who is described in an
inscription as "playing the harp for the good of their spirits every day."
Courtesy of the Walters Art Museum

> *Make holiday,*
> *Do not weary of it!*
> *Lo, none is allowed to take his goods with him,*
> *Lo, none who departs comes back again!*
>
> (Lichtheim, *Ancient Egyptian Literature,* Vol. 1, p. 197) (Fig. 90)

DANCE

In modern times dancing can be considered a recreational experience, an art form, or a religious expression, and dance can be
carried out by either amateurs or professionals. In ancient Egypt
the types of dance for which there is evidence were usually associated with religious rites and were accomplished by professionals
dedicated to the activity. Dancing is depicted in many representations, almost always connected with religious situations (Fig. 91).
The existence of a special group called the *muu* dancers illustrates a
specific example of the use of dance as a part of religious ritual. A

FIGURE 91   Dancers. Dynasty Six
             Tomb of Ptahhotep, Saqqara
             An energetic, high-kicking dance troupe apparently performing a
             carefully coordinated dance.
             Author's photograph

distinctive headdress identified these performers as they carried out
a rite at the funeral that was symbolic of the journey of the spirit to
the next life.

The performance of dancers as a part of temple ritual is well
documented by the depictions on a number of monuments. They
acted as participants in the temple rites and they also accompanied
the god's image when it was taken from its sanctuary and carried in
procession from one temple to another as a part of important festivals. A clear example of dancing as a part of religious observation
can be seen illustrated on the reliefs of the Red Chapel of Queen
Hatshepsut at Karnak, where a group of performers is shown in different stages of an acrobatic dance consisting of athletic back bends.
These are obviously not entertainers in the modern sense of the
word but rather more like ecstatic dancers who work themselves
into a trance-like state. The nearest modern equivalents are the Sufi
mystics, the so-called "whirling dervishes" whose repeated gyra-
tions transform or hypnotize them into a kind of ecstasy. In any case,

dances of various kinds were as integral to divine worship as prayer or offerings of food, clothing, or incense.

Like the musicians, dancers were both male and female, but they do not seem to have performed in mixed groups, as far as can be determined from the representations. Dancers could be shown as soloists, in pairs, or as part of line of performers, but the impression is that those with special talents or routines performed in front of, but still part of, the larger group, not unlike the soloists in a ballet who work before the ballet corps. Dancers were usually accompanied by others who clapped or beat time on a drum, tambourine, clappers, or the sistrum rattle.

The dancers involved in the rituals for the burial celebrated the mourning for the dead and the completion of the mummification process, the presentation of the food offerings to the spirit, and the idea of rebirth in the next existence. Dancers accompanied the funeral procession with the furnishings and provisions for the tomb. The *muu* dancers mentioned previously performed at the entrance to the tomb. Their special headdress made from papyrus stalks identified them as the ferrymen who were to transport the deceased across waters on the way to the underworld.

In addition to the *muu* dancers, another special type of participation in the funerary activities was carried out by dwarf dancers. They enacted a dance at the entrance to the tomb shaft that was a kind of farewell to the deceased. These are mentioned in texts, but so far depictions of them have not been found. Dwarfs or pygmies held a special place in the imagination of the ancient Egyptians because of their rarity, and they were often prized as dancers in contexts other than at the funeral. In Dynasty Six an inscription on the tomb of a nobleman named Harkhuf records the pleasure of King Pepy II when Harkhuf returned from an expedition from Nubia to the south.

> Come north to the residence at once! Hurry and bring with you this pygmy whom you brought from the land of the horizon-dwellers live, hale, and healthy, for the dances of the god, to gladden the heart, to delight the heart of King Neferkare [Pepy] who lives forever. (Lichtheim, *Ancient Egyptian Literature,* Vol. 1, p. 27)

This text certainly illustrates the importance of dance in ritual and as a spectator event. From the amount and variety of evidence of all types that has been preserved, it is very clear that music and dance were important parts of both the ordinary life and the special ceremonial activities of the Egyptians. It is only a pity that we will probably never know how the music sounded and that we have only a rudimentary idea of how the dances looked when they were performed, but it is clear that both were activities practiced throughout the history of ancient Egypt. Although the evidence seems to emphasize the use of both music and dance in formal ritual, it is hard to believe that they were not part of everyday activities shared by people in more casual circumstances.

Anderson, R. D. *Catalogue of Egyptian Antiquities in the British Museum*. Vol. 3, *Musical Instruments*. London: British Museum, 1976.

Foster, John. *Echoes of Egyptian Voices*. Norman: University of Oklahoma, 1992.

Manniche, Lise. *Music and Musicians in Ancient Egypt*. London: British Museum Press, 1991.

Strudwick, Nigel C. *Texts from the Pyramid Age*. Atlanta: Society of Biblical Literature, 2005.

Teeter, Emily. "Ritual Music" in *The Life of Meresamun: A Temple Singer in Ancient* Egypt, edited by Emily Teeter and Janet H. Johnson. Oriental Institute Museum Publications, No. 29. Chicago: Oriental Institute of the University of Chicago, 2009. Pp. 30–42.

15   Weapons and Armor

Clasping his shield he treads under foot,
No second blow needed to kill
None can escape his arrow,
None turn aside his bow.

FROM THE STORY OF SINUHE

Weapons of combat and self-defense developed side by side with the tools of the farmer and craftsman. As a result, at times some examples of tools and weapons are indistinguishable from each other. It is often difficult to decide whether a hatchet was meant as a carpentry tool or as a hand-to-hand weapon, just as a spear or javelin could equally be used in hunting or in battle. Even so, the weapons of the Egyptian military were basically simple and practical in design. From the prehistoric and Predynastic periods the only evidence that has been preserved of what may be classified as weapons are stone axes and projectile points. The blades of axes are much like those found in every prehistoric culture, simple, near ovoid, and originally handheld but later meant to be bound to a wooden handle with leather thongs or cord. Some of the early points for spears and arrows eventually exhibit a higher technology and have convex curves in the butt end, to allow a better fit and more secure attachment to a wooden or reed shaft.

Egyptian weapons can be divided into two general classes on the basis of how they were used and what the distance was between combatants. The first class includes the direct-contact hand-to-hand weapons for clubbing, stabbing, and cutting. The second is made up of those that function at a distance, including the spear or javelin, and others that aid in the launch of a projectile, such as the sling for pellets and bow for arrows. Clubbing and stabbing weapons were probably among the first to be developed, because they were simple and immediate. These were gradually supplemented but not replaced by the development of more advanced armament such as the sling and the bow (Fig. 92).

There are some other types that can be included in the repertoire of the earliest weapons, not so much from preserved examples but from illustrations on the ceremonial stone palettes of the Early

FIGURE 92   A troop of soldiers or marines armed with shields and spears. Dynasty
Eighteen
Wall relief from the mortuary temple of Hatshepsut at Deir el Bahri
The man on the far left is the commander of the troop; he is fol-
lowed by a person who carries his bow case.
Author's photograph

Dynastic Period. In these relief carvings hunters are armed with
curved throwing sticks and warriors are sometimes depicted with
bows and arrows that appear to be blunt-tipped. The blunt tips may
have been sharp chisel shapes that were as effective as more typical
pointed arrowheads. A parallel for them can be seen in much later
European crossbow bolts with similar tips. Even as the throwing
sticks continue as weapons throughout Dynastic history they become
the hunting implement of choice for bringing down birds in flight.
They are most commonly seen in depictions of bird hunting, but
occasionally soldiers are also shown carrying throwing sticks. This
object is sometimes misidentified as a boomerang, but they were not
designed to return in flight, and so this is obviously a misnomer.

Of all the early weapons developed by the Egyptians the mace
was the most direct, simple, and efficient. A mace is little more
than a club (from which it certainly evolved) with the addition of
compact weight on the striking end to make it more effective and
more lethal. The drilled stone mounted on a wooden handle was an

efficient stunning or killing device that was not difficult to make. Its production depended only on the technology used to drill a hole through a hard stone, and this resource for the manipulation of stone was developed early.

The basic design of the mace head took two forms; one was a "saucer" or disk shape and the other a "pear" or globular shape. While the saucer shape was also a kind of cutting weapon, the additional weight and crushing power provided by the pear shape probably gave it its continued popularity. In some cases the stone mace head, like the cosmetics palette, became an elaborate ritual object adorned with images of the ruler and used in ceremony. There seems to be no single weapon that lasted as long in Egyptian history as the mace in its various forms. It appears in artistic representations at the beginning of recorded history and was still in use throughout the existence of Dynastic Egypt. By Dynasty One it was already considered as a ceremonial weapon, as it is illustrated in the traditional depictions of the king, who is shown defeating his enemy with a stone-headed mace. This is the most obvious example of the use of the mace as it continued well into the Roman Period.

The range of sharp-edged weapons used by the Egyptians included knives, short swords, and the *khepesh*, a curved, scythe-like sword. By far the most commonly attested in the material record was the knife, used for both cutting and thrusting. Originally knives were made of flint or chert, stone that was abundantly found in the nearby deserts. Flint knives continued in use throughout Egyptian history, but as a tool for butchering and other domestic uses rather than as a weapon. As techniques of metallurgy developed knives were fashioned from copper and bronze, and it was not until late Dynasty Eighteen that iron knives even began to appear in Egypt. The outstanding example of an iron knife is one found in the tomb of Tutankhamun, probably made of iron imported from the Near East. It makes an interesting comparison with another knife of solid gold, also from his tomb. Whereas the newly introduced iron seems a more practical material compared with gold for actual use, both knives were probably considered as ceremonial objects.

Longer swords were not popular weapons in early Egypt, probably because they required a high level of metal technology to produce and were not particularly efficient for a military that for centuries had neither cavalry nor chariots. In the New Kingdom, when the horse-drawn chariot was introduced, the curved, scimitar-like *khepesh* became a popular weapon for military leaders. It is often shown wielded by the king as he rides into battle in his chariot.

From its design, it seems a formidable weapon for slashing and slicing. It is often described as a "sickle-shaped" sword, but the agricultural sickle has its cutting edge on the inside of the curve, whereas the *khepesh* has its cutting edge on the exterior or convex side.

The weapons of the ordinary Egyptian foot soldier were simple in the extreme and it is unlikely that they were ever equipped with anything more elaborate than a spear or an axe. On tomb and temple walls and in funerary models there are numerous representations of Egyptian troops armed with spears and shields, sometimes also with carrying axes and throwing sticks (Fig. 92).

The spear was one of the most practical instruments for hand-to-hand combat. It was also probably one of the oldest weapon types included in the Egyptian arsenal, descending, as it did, from stone-tipped hunting spears of the prehistoric period. In Pharaonic times the spear point was usually of copper or bronze, and the spearhead could be fashioned with a tang, designed to fit into the shaft, or socketed, to fit over the end of the shaft.

The battle axe also had a long and distinguished history in Egypt since it, too, developed out of prehistoric types. At first it closely resembled the carpenter's axe, with a blade approximately a half-circle in shape. It soon evolved into a longer projecting blade that was certainly more efficient in combat. Some axe blades could be decorated with openwork designs, but these were more likely intended as ceremonial or meant to have been given as awards. An additional type of axe-like cutting weapon had a shallow curved blade with a longer cutting edge fitted close to the handle. Representations of warriors with the different types of axe-like weapons often show them with the axe tucked into the belt when not in use.

Propelled weapons include the sling, javelin, and bow and arrow. The sling was the simplest to make, consisting only of cords and a pouch or pocket to hold the pebble projectile. The use of a sling requires considerable practice, which probably began in childhood, to judge from remains of slings found in child burials. Although the use of the sling in warfare is not so well attested as other devices, there are representations of soldiers using the sling, and furthermore it was also widely used in other Near Eastern cultures. The javelin is also not commonly attested, but this may be due to the possibility of mistaking depictions of it for examples of arrows in flight when it is represented in relief or painting.

Of all the weapons used by the Egyptian military, the bow and arrow was the most efficient – and probably the most deadly (Fig. 93). It was useful in hunting as well as in combat, so the skills acquired

FIGURE 93   **Soldiers with bows and arrows. Dynasty Eighteen**
Fragment from the temple of Deir el Bahri
This small fragment illustrates soldiers carrying their bows and arrows. The binding of the bowstring to the bow is clearly shown.
Courtesy of the Walters Art Museum

in one activity could be easily transferred to the other. Egyptian bows came in two distinct styles, one being in use somewhat later than the other. The earlier form was the simple bow or the "stave" bow, made from a single piece of wood. It has been suggested that this type of bow was capable of propelling an arrow around 600 feet, which would be roughly twice the length of an American football field. Accuracy at that distance would be negligible, but a group of bowman shooting at the same time would make up in blanketing quantity what was lacking in precision. The second and later type of bow was introduced, probably from the east, during the Second Intermediate Period. This was the composite bow, the product of a lamination technique where wood was combined with animal sinew and horn. Although this type of bow required considerable skill to make, the resulting weapon was stronger, obviously more lethal, and had an increase in range of about one third. Due to increased time and skill involved in its manufacture it was probably the deluxe weapon of the elite and of royalty.

Arrows were made of reeds and tipped with stone, bone, ivory, or metal arrowheads. "Fletching," the technique of adding feathers to the shaft of an arrow, was necessary to control and direct flight. The additional equipment of the bowman sometimes included an arm guard to protect against the bowstring. Quivers to contain extra arrows and bow cases also were used, but most infantrymen are shown carrying loose arrows, and the bow cases are usually depicted as an accessory to a chariot.

Defensive equipment included the parrying stick, carried in the hand not holding a weapon and used to ward off the thrusts or blows of the opponent. More elaborate defense was provided by the shield. From preserved models and depictions in tombs and on the walls of coffins the typical shield was made of dappled cowhide stretched on a wood frame. The shape was the opposite of the typical later European shield. The Egyptian type was pointed at the top and flat across the bottom. This enabled the foot soldier to place his shield on the ground and crouch behind it to ward off enemy projectiles. Ceremonial shields, such as the ones found in the tomb of Tutankhamun, were often of openwork wood, elaborately painted or gilded.

Body armor was not universally employed by the Egyptians, but when it was used it consisted mainly of shirts and corselets made of overlapping small plates or scales of metal or hard leather. Some fragments of such armor have been found and some images of the god Amun show him with what is described as an "imbricated corselet," which may represent body armor. Helmets are virtually unknown except in scenes representing the king or foreigners. The blue crown of the king seems to have been a helmet for battle, and it is often depicted as having small circular studs or plates, but that is the one instance of a well-attested headgear that may have been for protection.

Some rare compositions show what must have been the inventories of the royal armory and include piles of bows and arrows, khepesh swords, and even chariots. In Middle Kingdom coffins in the so-called frieze of offerings, bows and arrows and quivers are included among the objects deemed needed for the good of the spirit in the next life. In addition to the painted representation in the Middle Kingdom tombs, models of cowhide shields and arrows or javelins with their quivers are often included, and shields are represented painted as if they were hanging on the coverings of the cabins in many Middle Kingdom boat models. Two unusual models of army troops depict Egyptian and Nubian soldiers with their typical arms, the Egyptians with spears and shields and the Nubians with bows and arrows.

The craftsmen who produced weaponry were probably not so different from those who made furniture and other useful objects;

the skills were somewhat interchangeable. Little special skill was required to make spears and shields or bow and arrows. The records of military leaders like Thutmosis III and Ramesses II are evidence that the Egyptian soldier could hold his own in combat with such simple equipment. It was only with the wider development of metallurgy in the first millennium BCE in the Middle East that Egyptian troops found themselves at a serious disadvantage when faced with an enemy clad in metal armor.

Hoffmeier, James K. "Military: Material" in *Oxford Encyclopedia of Ancient Egypt*, edited by Donald B. Redford. Oxford: Oxford University Press, 2001. Vol. 2, pp. 406–412.

McDermott, Bridget. *Warfare in Ancient Egypt*. Stroud: Sutton Publishing, 2004.

Partridge, Robert B. *Fighting Pharaohs: Weapons and Warfare in Ancient Egypt*. Manchester: Peartree, 2002.

Petrie, W. M. F. *Tools and Weapons*. London: British School of Archaeology in Egypt, 1917.

Yadin, Yigael. *The Art of Warfare in Biblical Lands*. New York: McGraw-Hill, 1963.

Conclusions

Any assessment of the material world of ancient Egypt has to include
a catalog of the resources immediately available to the dwellers in
the Nile valley. On the most basic level the Egyptians possessed
the essential ingredients for survival from the beginning of their
culture – a constant supply of water and at least the potential for
gathering and eventually growing foodstuffs. In addition to collecting food from the native plant materials they had the possibilities of
supplementing their diet by hunting and trapping. Eventual guar-
anties of continued supplies were provided by the domestication of
animals and the gradual development of agriculture. In the transi-
tion from the state of hunting and gathering to organized agriculture and animal husbandry, the utilization of local resources for the
production of shelter, clothing, and tools had to be understood and
utilized.

The Nile valley and the delta were rich in some basic material
assets and lacking in others. One of the most abundant (and obvious) resources was the rich earth that was renewed each year. Not
only did it make the cultivation of crops, particularly varieties of
grain, a relatively simple operation, but it provided building materials that were readily available and simple to work with. However,
an extensive supply of wood for construction was not one of these
resources.

In the early beginnings of settlement and shelter building, the
type of construction termed "wattle and daub" was utilized to
take advantage of both mud and clay in combination with the limited structural elements provided by the local vegetation. In this
well-attested technique the framework or basic structures were
erected using reeds, rushes, or sticks filled in with rammed and patted earth. This kind of building provided a basic dwelling with a
limited amount of protection against both heat and cold.

It was an important step from wattle and daub to the use of pre-pared cubic units made of the same local earth, a method of construction termed mud brick architecture. The idea that the earth or mud could be formed into regular shapes and cured to a degree of hardness in the sun was an important innovation that would continue to be utilized throughout the history of the culture and is still used to the present. This technique of construction was particularly adaptable to Egypt, with its limited amount of rainfall. The additional innovations of plastered walls and hard-packed or stamped floors helped to create living spaces that were cleaner, more sanitary, and incidentally more attractive.

In addition to its use for house building, mud brick was the basic material in the construction of precinct and perimeter walls, defensive installations and fortresses, and in some pyramids that were not completely made of stone. The thick walls surrounding the precinct of Amun, at Karnak, stand as a major example of the massive use of the material, consisting as they do of mud bricks numbering in the hundreds of thousands. An additional major use of mud brick was in the construction of the temporary ramps used in large-scale building operations. These are illustrated in tomb paintings and attested to by the remains of some actual ramps still in place. Together the paintings and existing examples provide the best evidence for the methods of construction of most of the stone monuments of Egypt.

The rich earth of the valley and the delta, with its annual renewal, provided the basis for the continued production of staple grain crops of emmer wheat and barley from the early Predynastic Period throughout the history of Egypt. The cultivation of a wide range of fruits and vegetables is also attested early in Egyptian history. From the pictorial evidence of tomb walls alone it is fairly evident that in normal times of consistent yearly floods the populace was sustained with a regular and varied supply of food.

The ancient Egyptians were ingenious and resourceful in the varied uses of the natural resources available to them. Common clay was probably the outstanding example, with its many different applications. The fiber derived from the ubiquitous papyrus plant was used to produce baskets, sandals, mats, and screens, as well as being processed to provide the signature writing material of the culture. To cite a similar example, readily available animal hides were used to make water skins, drumheads, bellows, and sandals, as well as some forms of clothing, armor, and warriors' protective shields when stretched on a frame. From the earliest times the production of the flax plant supplied the basic source for both textiles and cordage.

It seems that no resource was limited to a single use: the variations possible were limited only by the degree of ingenuity of the worker or craftsman.

It is acknowledged that some of the materials and the technology to use them were not native to Egypt and were imported primarily from western Asia and Mesopotamia. Bronze was somewhat late in coming to Egypt and the use of iron even later. The effective manufacture of glass for vessels or containers was practiced only for a period in the New Kingdom, probably based on the knowledge and techniques of foreign craftsmen. The horse as a beast of transport and the wheeled vehicle were not in common use until the New Kingdom, but the Egyptians had managed without them until they were introduced from outside the country. Since there was no source of large timber in the Nile valley, wood, primarily cedar, was brought from the Lebanon throughout most of Egyptian history.

In contrast to materials and crafts imported from abroad, the Egyptians maintained thriving industries in the production of faience and jewelry made from precious metals and semiprecious stones. The materials for faience were easily available locally; however the gold, silver, and some of the colored stones for jewelry had to be obtained from the south or the east. The Egyptians were also in the forefront of ship- and boatbuilding in antiquity, and their manipulation of stone in the construction of temples, tombs, and pyramids was without equal in the ancient world. Their array of tools was of the simplest and most elementary designs possible, but they could still level and orient a construction site with great accuracy, wrench hard stone of immense size from quarries, manufacture elegant furniture, and clothe themselves in fashionable linen garments. The material world of the ancient Egyptians was based on an uncomplicated use of the materials that were, for the most part, close at hand or easily obtained through trade.

As has been noted we are fortunate to have so much evidence about materials and activities of the ancient Egyptians, even if it is somewhat slanted to reflect the lives of special classes. The long history of Egyptian civilization should also automatically make us cautious about generalizing about almost anything the Egyptians did. Still, the picture of the material world of the Egyptians is rich with detail and filled with information. We are indebted to the archaeologists, scholars, and scientists who have labored over the retrieval, analysis, and interpretation of the artifacts that form the basis of our understanding. The discipline of Egyptology is only a little more than two hundred years old, and new discoveries are constantly being made, both in excavations in the field and in scholarly research. The study of ancient history is far from static, and the appreciation of ancient Egypt and the Egyptians can only become more satisfying as the picture becomes more complete.

SOURCES OF CHAPTER HEADING QUOTATIONS

Introduction: Herodotus, *Histories*, Book II, 35, trans. A. D. Godley, Loeb Classical Library, Cambridge, 1920

1. Geography and Geology: The Land: Diodorus Siculus, *Histories*, Book I, 36, trans. C. H. Oldfather, Loeb Classical Library, Cambridge, 1968
2. Brief Outline of Egyptian History: Sir Alan Gardiner, *Egypt of the Pharaohs,* Oxford, 1964
3. Study of The Material World of Ancient Egypt: Adolf Erman, *Life in Ancient Egypt,* trans. H. M. Tirard, London and New York, 1894
4. Dress and Personal Adornment: "The Prayers of Paheri," M. Lichtheim, *Ancient Egyptian Literature*, Vol. 2, p. 16, Berkeley, 1976
   "The Instruction of Amenemope," M. Lichtheim, *Ancient Egyptian Literature*, Vol. 2, p. 157, Berkeley, 1976
5. Housing and Furniture: From the tomb of Rekhmire in Thebes, quoted in T. G. H. James, *Pharaoh's People*, London, 1984
6. Food and Drink: From a memorandum of payment owed, quoted in T. G. H. James, *Pharaoh's People,* London, 1984
7. Hygiene and Medicine: From a letter, quoted in T. G. H. James, *Pharaoh's People,* London, 1984
8. Containers of Clay and Stone: From the "Satire of the Trades," M. Lichtheim, *Ancient Egyptian Literature*, Vol. 1, p. 186, Berkeley, 1973
9. Tools and Weapons: From the "Satire of the Trades," T. G. H. James, *Pharaoh's People,* London, 1984
10. Basketry, Rope, Matting: From a letter, Edward Wente, *Letters from Ancient Egypt* (No. 231, Dynasty Nineteen), Atlanta, 1990

11. Faience and Glass: From a stela dated to early Dynasty Nineteen, catalog No. 166, in *Gifts of the Nile: Ancient Egyptian Faience,* Providence, 1998

12. Transportation: Caption to a tomb scene, Nigel C. Strudwick, *Texts from the Pyramid Age,* p. 417, Atlanta, 2005

13. Sport and Games: Excerpt from the "Sphinx Stela," M. Lichtheim, *Ancient Egyptian Literature*, Vol. 2, p. 41, Berkeley, 1976

BIBLIOGRAPHY

BIBLIOGRAPHICAL NOTE

There have been many attempts to describe daily life in ancient Egypt. Sir John Gardner Wilkinson's *Manners and Customs of the Ancient Egyptians* (1837–41) and Adolf Erman's *Life in Ancient Egypt,* translated into English in 1894, were among the first attempts to approach the subject in depth, and both have had a lasting influence on the modern appreciation of life in the land of the Pharaohs. Since this book has had as its major concern the material world of ancient Egypt it has relied heavily on *Ancient Egyptian Materials and Technology,* edited by Paul T. Nicholson and Ian Shaw, Cambridge, 2000; on *Egypt's Golden Age: The art of living in the New Kingdom 1558–1085 B.C.,* edited by Brovarski, Doll, and Freed, Boston, 1982; as well as the *Oxford Encyclopedia of Ancient Egypt*, edited by Donald B. Redford, Oxford, 2001. *Ancient Egyptian Materials and Industries,* by Alfred Lucas and J. R. Harris, London, 1962, also remains a valuable resource to the materials of ancient Egypt that has not yet been completely supplanted by recent research.

Abt, Jeffrey. *American Egyptologist: The Life of James Henry Breasted and the Creation of His Oriental Institute.* Chicago: University of Chicago Press, 2011.

Aldred, Cyril. *Jewels of the Pharaohs: Egyptian Jeweler of The Dynastic Period.* London: Thames and Hudson, 1971.

Allen, James P. *The Art of Medicine in Ancient Egypt.* New York: Metropolitan Museum of Art, 2005.

Anderson, R. D. *Catalogue of Egyptian Antiquities in the British Museum.* Vol. 3, *Musical Instruments.* London: British Museum Publications, 1976.

Arnold, Dieter. *Building in Egypt: Pharaonic Stone Masonry.* New York: Oxford University Press, 1991.

Aston, Barbara G. *Ancient Egyptian Stone Vessels: Materials and Forms.* Heidelberg: Heidelberger Orientverlag, 1994.

Bagnall, Roger S. *Egypt in Late Antiquity.* Princeton, NJ: Princeton University Press, 1993.

The Oxford Handbook of Papyrology. Oxford: Oxford University Press, 2009.

Baines, John, and Jaromir Malek. *Atlas of Ancient Egypt.* New York: Facts on File Publications, 1980.

Baker, Hollis S., and Gordon Russell. *Furniture in the Ancient World.* London: Connoisseur, 1966.

Belzoni, Giovanni. *Narrative of the Operations and Recent Discoveries Within the Pyramids, Temples, Tombs and Excavations in Egypt and Nubia.* London: John Murray, 1820.

Bourriau, Janine. *Umm El-Ga'ab: Pottery from the Nile Valley Before the Arab Conquest.* Cambridge: Cambridge University Press, 1981.

Bowman, Alan Keir. *Egypt After the Pharaohs.* London: British Museum Publications, 1986.

Breasted, Charles. *Pioneer to the Past: The Story of James Henry Breasted.* New York: Scribner, 1943.

Brovarskie, E., S. K. Doll, and R. Freed. *Egypt's Golden Age, the Art of Living in the New Kingdom, 1558–1085 B.C.: Catalogue of the exhibition.* Boston: Museum of Fine Arts, 1982.

Butzer, Karl W. *Early Hydraulic Civilization in Egypt: A Study in Cultural Ecology.* Chicago: University of Chicago Press, 1976.

Champollion, J. F. *Monuments de'Égypte et de la Nubie: notices descriptive, 1835–47.* Paris: Firmin Didot Frères, 1835.

Connor, David. *Abydos: Egypt's First Pharaohs and the Cult of Osiris.* Cairo: American University in Cairo Press, 2009.

Darby, William J. *Food: The Gift of Osiris.* London: Academic Press, 1977.

Davies, W. V. *Catalogue of Egyptian Antiquities in the British Museum.* Vol. 7, *Tools and Weapons.* London: Published for the Trustees of the British Museum by British Museum Publications, 1987.

Decker, Wolfgang. "Sports" in *The Oxford Encyclopedia of Ancient Egypt.* Oxford: Oxford University Press, 2001. Vol. 3, pp. 310–314.
Sports and Games of Ancient Egypt. New Haven: Yale University Press, 1992.

Diodorus Siculus. *The Histories.* Cambridge, MA: Harvard University Press, 1970.

Erman, Adolf. *Life in Ancient Egypt.* London: Macmillan, 1894.

Fagan, Brian M. *The Rape of the Nile: Tomb Robbers, Tourists, and Archaeologists in Egypt.* New York: Scribner, 1975.

Filer, Joyce. *Disease.* Austin: University of Texas Press, 1996.

Foster, John L. *Echoes of Egyptian Voices: An Anthology of Ancient Egyptian Poetry.* Norman: University of Oklahoma Press, 1992.

Gardiner, Alan H. *Egypt of the Pharaohs: An introduction.* Oxford: Clarendon Press, 1961.

Geller, Jeremy. "From Prehistory to History: Beer in Egypt" in *The Followers of Horus: Studies Dedicated to Michael Allen Hoffman, 1944–1990,* edited by Renée Friedman and Barbara Adams. Oxford: Oxbow, 1992. Pp. 19–26.

Greener, Leslie. *The Discovery of Egypt: Leslie Greener*. London: Cassell, 1966.

Grimal, Nicolas. *A History of Ancient Egypt*. Oxford: Blackwell, 1992.

Halioua, Bruno, and Bernard Ziskind. *Medicine in the Days of the Pharaohs*. Cambridge, MA: Belknap Press of Harvard University Press, 2005.

Hall, Rosalind. "Garments in the Petrie Museum of Archaeology." *Textile History* 13 (1) (1982), 27–45.

Hall, Rosalind M. *Egyptian Textiles*. Aylesbury: Shire, 1986.

Hepper, F. N. *Pharaoh's Flowers: The Botanical Treasures of Tutankhamun*. London: H.M.S.O., 1990.

Herodotus. *The Histories*. Cambridge, MA: Harvard Univ. Press. 1966.

Hodges, Henry. *Technology in the Ancient World*. New York: Knopf. 1970.

Hoffmeier, James K. "Military: Material" in *The Oxford Encyclopedia of Ancient Egypt*, edited by Donald B. Redford. Oxford: Oxford University Press, 2001. Pp. 406–412.

Hope, Colin A. *Egyptian Pottery*. Aylesbury: Shire, 1987.

James, T. G. H. *The British Museum Concise Introduction to Ancient Egypt*. Ann Arbor: University of Michigan Press, 2005.

   An Introduction to Ancient Egypt. New York: Harper & Row, 1990.

Jenkins, Nancy. *The Boat Beneath the Pyramid*. New York: Holt, Rinehart and Winston, 1980.

Kees, Hermann. *Ancient Egypt: A Cultural Topography*. Phoenix ed. Chicago: University of Chicago Press, 1977.

Kemp, Barry J. *Ancient Egypt: Anatomy of a Civilization*. London: Routledge, 1989.

Kendall, Timothy. "Games" in *The Oxford Encyclopedia of Ancient Egypt*, edited by Donald B. Redford. Oxford: Oxford University Press, 2001. Vol. 2, pp. 1–3.

Killen, Geoffrey. *Egyptian Woodworking and Furniture*. Princes Risborough: Shire, 1994.

Langner, Lawrence. *The Importance of Wearing Clothes*. Rev. ed. Los Angeles: Elysium Growth Press, 1991.

Lepsius, Karl Richard. *Denkmaeler aus Aegypten und Aethiopien nach den Zeichnungen der von Seiner Majestät dem Koenige von Preussen, Friedrich Wilhelm IV., nach diesen Ländern gesendeten, und in den Jahren 1842–1845 ausgeführten wissenschaftlichen Expedition auf Befehl Seiner Majestät*. 13 vols. Berlin: Nicolaische Buchhandlung. 1849 (Reprinted Genève: Éditions de Belles-Lettres, 1972).

Littauer, M. A., and J. H. Crouwel. *Chariots and Related Equipment from the Tomb of Tutankhamun*. Oxford: Griffith Institute, 1985.

Manniche, Lise. *An Ancient Egyptian Herbal*. Updated ed. London: British Museum, 2006.

   Music and Musicians in Ancient Egypt. London: British Museum Press, 1991.

McDermott, Bridget. *Warfare in Ancient Egypt*. Stroud: Sutton, 2004.

Meeks, Dimitri. "Dance" in *The Oxford Encyclopedia of Ancient Egypt*, edited by Donald B. Redford. Oxford: Oxford University Press, 2001. Vol. 1, pp. 356–360.

Mendeles, Mikhal. *Perfumes and Cosmetics in the Ancient World*. Jerusalem: Israel Museum, 1989.

Nicholson, Paul T. *Egyptian Faience and Glass*. Princes Risborough: Shire, 1993.

Nicholson, Paul T., and Ian Shaw. *Ancient Egyptian Materials and Technology*. Cambridge: Cambridge University Press, 2000.

Nunn, John F. *Ancient Egyptian Medicine*. London: British Museum, 1997.

Ogden, Jack. "Metals" in *Ancient Egyptian Materials and Technology*, edited by Paul T. Nicholson and Ian Shaw. Cambridge: Cambridge University Press, 2000. Pp. 148–176.

Partridge, Robert. *Transport in Ancient Egypt*. London: Rubicon, 1996.

Partridge, Robert B. *Fighting Pharaohs: Weapons and Warfare in Ancient Egypt*. Manchester: Peartree Pub., 2002.

Peck, William H. "The constant lure" in *Ancient Egypt: Discovering Its Splendors*, edited by W. K. Simpson. Washington, DC: National Geographic Society, 1977.

Petrie, William M. Flinders. *Tools and Weapons*. London: School of Archaeology in Egypt, 1917.

Redford, Donald B. *The Oxford Encyclopedia of Ancient Egypt*. Oxford: Oxford University Press, 2001.

Sampsell, Bonnie M. *A Traveler's Guide to the Geology of Egypt*. Cairo: American University in Cairo Press, 2003.

Samuel, Delwen. "Archaeology of Ancient Egyptian Beer." *Journal of the American Society of Brewing Chemists* 54 (1), 3–12, 1996.

Scheel, Bernd. *Egyptian Metalworking and Tools*. Aylesbury: Shire, 1989.

Shaw, Ian. *The Oxford History of Ancient Egypt*. Oxford: Oxford University Press, 2000.

Spencer, A. Jeffrey. *Brick Architecture in Ancient Egypt*. Warminster: Aris and Phillips, 1979.

Store, Anthony. *Music and the Mind*. New York: Free Press, 1992.

Strudwick, Nigel. *Texts from the Pyramid Age*. Atlanta: Society of Biblical Literature, 2005.

Teeter, Emily. "Techniques and Terminology of Rope-Making in Ancient Egypt." *The Journal of Egyptian Archaeology* 73 (1987), 71–77.

Teeter, Emily, and Janet H. Johnson. *The Life of Meresamun: A Temple Singer in Ancient Egypt*. Chicago: Oriental Institute of the University of Chicago, 2009.

Touny, A. D., and Steffen Wenig. *Sport in Ancient Egypt*. Leipzig: Edition Leipzig, 1969.

Tyldesley, Joyce Ann. *Egyptian Games and Sports*. Princes Risborough: Shire, 2007.

Vinson, Steve. *Egyptian Boats and Ships*. Princes Risborough: Shire, 1994.

Vogelsang-Eastwood, Gillian. *Patterns for Ancient Egyptian Clothing*. Leiden: Stichting Textile Research Center, 1992.

"Textiles" in *Ancient Egyptian Materials and Technology*, edited by Paul T. Nicholson and Ian Shaw. Cambridge: Cambridge University Press, 2000. Pp. 268–298.

Pharaonic Egyptian Clothing. Leiden: E.J. Brill, 1993.

Wendrich, Willemina Z. "Basketry" in *Ancient Egyptian Materials and Technology*, edited by Paul T. Nicholson and Ian Shaw. Cambridge: Cambridge University Press, 2000. Pp. 254–267.

Wente, Edward Frank, and Edmund S. Meltzer. *Letters from Ancient Egypt*. Atlanta, GA: Scholars Press, 1990.

Wilkinson, John Gardner. *Manners and Customs of the Ancient Egyptians*. London: John Murray, 1837

The Egyptians in the Time of the Pharaohs. London: Bradbury and Evans, 1857

Wilson, Hilary. *Egyptian Food and Drink*. Aylesbury: Shire, 1988.

Wilson, John A. *Thousands of Years: An Archaeologist's Search for Ancient Egypt*. New York: Scribner, 1972.

Wilson, John Albert. *Signs & Wonders Upon Pharaoh; a History of American Egyptology*. Chicago: University of Chicago Press, 1964.

Wilson, John A. *Thousands of years; an archaeologist's search for ancient Egypt*. New York: Scribner, 1972.

Yadin, Yigael. *The Art of Warfare in Biblical Lands*. New York: McGraw-Hill, 1963.

INDEX